Neue Freunde

Erster Teil

HBJ
Foreign Language Programs

GERMAN

- **Neue Freunde**
  Level 1
  - Erster Teil
  - Zweiter Teil
  - Dritter Teil

- **Wir, die Jugend**
  Level 2

- **Unsere Welt**
  Level 3

Neue Freunde

Erster Teil

HBJ HARCOURT BRACE JOVANOVICH, PUBLISHERS

Orlando   San Diego   Chicago   Dallas

Printed in the United States of America
ISBN 0-15-383490-0

PHOTO CREDITS: All photos by George Winkler/Harbrace except: **1:** Horst Munzig/Anne Hamann; **2:** (tr circle)Hans Madej/Bilderberg; (c)Ossi Baumeister/Anne Hamann; (br)Hans Madej/Bilderberg; **3:** (insert)Ossi Baumeister/Anne Hamann; **4:** (c)Ossi Baumeister/Anne Hamann; (b)Walter Schmitz/Bilderberg;(insert)J. Messerschmidt/Stock Market; **5:** (t)R. Betzler/Anne Hamann; (bl)Margot Granitsas/Photo Researchers;(br)Guido Mangold/Anne Hamann; **6:** (t–insert)Andrej Reiser/Bilderberg; (c)Milan Horacek/Bilderberg; (b)Andrej Reiser/Bilderberg; (insert)Andrej Reiser/Bilderberg; **7:** (tl)Ossi Baumeister/Anne Hamann; (br)Alexas Urba/Stock Market; **8:** (t)Luis Villota/Stock Market; (t–insert)Guido Mangold/Anne Hamann; (b)Werner Müller/Peter Arnold; (b–insert)Werner Müller/Peter Arnold; **9:** (tl)Steve Vidler/Leo de Wys; (tr)G. Davies/Leo de Wys; (bl)Dagmar Fabricius/Stock Boston; (br)Steve Vidler/Leo de Wys; **10:** (tr)Ossi Baumeister/Anne Hamann; (br—2nd from bottom)Bob Krist/Leo de Wys; **11:** (tl)Culver; (tr)Bettmann Archive; (cl)Scala/Art Resource; (cr)Giraudon/Art Resource; (bl)Bettmann Archive; (bc)Ken Hawkins/Sygma; (br)Marburg/Art Resource; **12:** (tl)Culver; (tr)Bettmann Archive; (cl)Culver; (cr)Bettmann Archive; (bl)German Information Center; (br)Bettmann Archive; **13:** (tl insert)H. Newton/Sygma; (t)J.L. Atlan/Sygma; (bl)Sygma; (bc)H. Newton/Sygma; (br)Culver; **14:** (b)Adam Woolfitt/Woodfin Camp;

continued on page 155

Writer
George Winkler

Contributing Writer
Margrit Meinel Diehl

Editorial Advisors

Robert L. Baker
Middlebury College
Middlebury, VT

Pat Barr-Harrison
Prince George's County
   Schools
Landover, MD

Ellen N. Benson
Northwestern High School
Hyattsville, MD

Ann Beusch
Hood College
Frederick, MD

Guy Capelle
Université de Paris VIII
Paris, France

Inge D. Halpert
Columbia University
New York, NY

Charles R. Hancock
Ohio State University
Columbus, OH

William Jassey
Norwalk Board of Education
Norwalk, CT

Dora Kennedy
Prince George's County
   Schools
Landover, MD

Claire J. Kramsch
Massachusetts Institute of
   Technology
Cambridge, MA

Ilonka Schmidt Mackey
Université Laval
Québec, Canada

William F. Mackey
Université Laval
Québec, Canada

Consultants and Reviewers

Wolfgang M. Baur
Loyola High School
Los Angeles, CA

Dorothea Bruschke
Parkway School District
Chesterfield, MO

Edeltraut Ehrlich
Markgräfler Gymnasium
Müllheim, FRG

Eileen Johannsen
Nicolet High School
Glendale, WI

Gisela Schwab
Ramapo High School
Franklin Lakes, NJ

Field-Test Teachers

Cecilia Brisentine,
Baltimore, MD

Dieter Dose
Accompsett Intermediate
   School
Smithtown, NY

Maureen Helinski
Andover Senior High School
Baltimore, MD

Barbara Hoess
Springfield High School
Erdenheim, PA

Carol Paezold Kochefko
Staples High School
Westport, CT

Robert K. Krebs
Smithtown High School West
Smithtown, NY

Rita Leonardi
Brian McMahon High School
South Norwalk, CT

Lynn Preston
Haddon Township High
   School
Westmont, NJ

Renate Wilson
Frederick High School
Frederick, MD

ACKNOWLEDGMENTS

We wish to express our thanks to the students pictured in this textbook and to the parents who allowed us to photograph these young people in their homes and in other places. We also thank the teachers and the families who helped us find these young people; the school administrators who allowed us to photograph the students in their schools; and the merchants who permitted us to photograph the students in their stores and other places of business.

YOUNG PEOPLE
Christof Augenstein, Nadja Balawi, Jens Balcke, Anja Bayertz, Jutta Bolanz, Michael Böse, Bernhard Braun, Matthias Braun, Daniela Broghammer, Christine Cochius, Margit Dastl, Josef Eisenhofer, Hans-Georg Esser, Natalie Fiedler, Jörg Flechtner, Michael Gipp, Nicolas Golubvic, Olaf Günter, Anja Hauswirth, Herman Holst, Marina Hrusha, Mona Johannsen, Daniele Käser, Daniel Kehl, Katja Keiling, Josef Kerscher, Stefan Kiefer, Katja Kramer, Birte Kreuzer, Matthias Kroll, Eva Leonhardt, Michaela Mayer, Jörg Mast, Giuseppe Matano, Philipp Nedel, Wiebke Nedel, Meike Nimmermann, Sven Nipken, Gupse Özkan, Kathrin Pahulycz, Michael Pertsch, Christian Risch, Bruno Schmidlin, Ulrike Schwemmer, Tobias Steinhoff, Claudia Stromberger, Friederike Thyssen, Hendrik Wermier, Rita Werner, Christian Wild

TEACHERS AND FAMILIES
Fritz and Marianne Brunner, Dornbirn; Burkhardt and Edeltraut Ehrlich, Müllheim; Ernst and Christine Hofer, Wien; Hartmut and Sabine Nedel, Neuss; Karl-Uwe and Renate Sperling; Niebüll; Marianne Sperling, München

CONTENTS

INTRODUCTION
German and You 1

ERSTER TEIL

COMMUNICATIVE FUNCTIONS	GRAMMAR	CULTURE
Socializing • Saying hello and goodbye • Greeting adults		Popular first names of boys and girls Meeting and greeting people
Exchanging information • Asking and giving names • Asking who someone is	The definite articles **der, die, das**	German family names and German names in the United States
Exchanging information • Asking someone's age and telling your age **Counting** • Learning the numbers from 0 to 20	The personal pronouns and the verb **sein**	How numerals are written and how they are signaled by hand
Exchanging information • Asking where someone else is from and telling where you're from **Socializing** • Saying you don't understand and asking for clarification	Asking and answering questions	A map of the German-speaking countries showing where our friends live Using the **Sie**-form
Recombining communicative functions, grammar, and vocabulary		Writing a letter in German to a pen pal
Reading for practice and pleasure		Geography of German-speaking countries Greetings on postcards

COMMUNICATIVE FUNCTIONS	GRAMMAR	CULTURE
Exchanging information • Telling how you get to school	The verb **kommen**	How students get to school
Exchanging information • Asking about prices of school supplies **Socializing** • Saying please, thank you, and you're welcome • Getting someone's attention	The definite articles **der, die, das** Noun plurals **Was kostet—was kosten** The pronouns **er, sie, es,** and **sie** (plural)	German currency and how to read prices The concept of grammatical gender
Exchanging information • Giving information about your class schedule • Telling time	The verb **haben**	System of scheduling classes Subjects taught in German schools
Exchanging information • Talking about homework and grades **Expressing feelings and emotions** • Responding to good news and to bad news		System of grading
Recombining communicative functions, grammar, and vocabulary		A German exchange student talks about himself
Reading for practice and pleasure		

COMMUNICATIVE FUNCTIONS	GRAMMAR	CULTURE
Exchanging information • Asking someone about his or her interests	Using the **du**-form Using the **ihr**-form The present tense	Popular sports and hobbies Three ways of saying *you* in German
Exchanging information • Talking about when and how often you do your various sports and activities	Word order: verb in second place	How young people spend their free time
Expressing attitudes and opinions • Asking for an opinion; expressing enthusiasm or the lack of it • Expressing surprise, agreement, and disagreement **Expressing feelings and emotions** • Expressing likes, dislikes, and preferences	**gern, lieber, am liebsten, nicht gern**	Student survey: preferred sports activities
Recombining communicative functions, grammar, and vocabulary		Olympic sports symbols Pen-pal section from a magazine for young people
Reading for practice and pleasure		What young people read A computer hobbyist
Reviewing communicative functions, grammar, and vocabulary		Excerpts from a school newspaper

FOR REFERENCE

MAPS

GETTING TO KNOW YOUR TEXTBOOK

WILLKOMMEN

Some of us are fortunate enough to be able to learn a new language by living in another country, but most of us are not. We begin learning the language and getting acquainted with the foreign culture in a classroom with the help of a teacher and a textbook. Your textbook can be a reliable guide if you know how to use it effectively. The following pages will help you get to know **Neue Freunde** (*New Friends*) and its various features.

Neue Freunde has been divided into three separate books. The first book (**Erster Teil**) contains Units 1–4; the second book (**Zweiter Teil**) contains Units 5–8; the third book (**Dritter Teil**) contains Units 9–12.

Neue Freunde

- **Erster Teil** (Book 1)
  Zweiter Teil (Book 2)
  Dritter Teil (Book 3)

INTRODUCTION

Who speaks German? Where is German spoken? Where did the language come from? Why should I learn it? How can I learn it well? You'll find the answers to these questions in English, illustrated with colorful photographs, in the Introduction, which begins on page 1.

INTRODUCTION
German and You

Welcome to the German-speaking world! During the coming year you will learn to understand, speak, read, and write German in a variety of situations. You will also learn more about the German-speaking world outside your classroom: daily life, customs, traditions, music, art, science, and history. As you begin your travels through the German-speaking world, here's wishing you . . .

Viel Glück!
Good luck!

In this introduction you will learn about:

 1 Germany: a pictorial view

 2 the German-speaking countries

 3 German in the United States

 4 German, English, and other languages

 5 German and your future career

 6 suggestions for studying German

1

PART OPENER

There are twelve units in Neue Freunde, grouped in three Parts. Each Part contains three units and a review unit based on them. At the beginning of each Part, you'll see an illustrated table of contents like the one shown here. It will tell you the number, title, and opening page of each unit (Kapitel) and give you a brief preview, in English, of each unit's theme and content.

KAPITEL **1**
Neue Freunde

UNIT OPENER

Nine units in your textbook present new material. Each of these units opens the same way. Before you begin a unit, examine its two opening pages. First scan the photos—they'll give you an idea of what the unit is about. Next read the introductory paragraph—it sets the theme and provides information about the life and customs of German-speaking people. Finally, look at the outline of the unit. Read the objectives of each section carefully. They'll tell you specifically what you'll be learning to communicate.

REVIEW UNIT OPENER

Review is essential to learning a second language. It's good to stop now and then to ask yourself what you've learned and, more importantly, to practice your new skills in different situations. That's just what each review unit (Wiederholungskapitel) will help you do. There is one review unit at the end of each Part—three in the book. In the review unit you'll be introduced to a new theme and

Meeting new friends is exciting, especially when they speak another language. When you meet someone who speaks German, you need to know how to say hello and goodbye, how to find out a little about the person, and how to tell a bit about yourself. In this unit you will meet five new friends your own age from the Federal and Democratic Republics of Germany, from Austria, and Switzerland.

In this unit you will:

SECTION **A**	say hello and say goodbye
SECTION **B**	ask someone's name and give your name
SECTION **C**	ask someone's age and tell your age, count from 1 to 20
SECTION **D**	ask and tell where someone is from
TRY YOUR SKILLS	use what you've learned
ZUM LESEN	read for practice and pleasure

setting, but you won't have to learn any new vocabulary, grammar, or communicative functions (language uses). Just concentrate on using what you've already studied in new and interesting ways.

KAPITEL **12**

Ferien in Österreich

Wiederholungskapitel

SECTIONS

With the exception of the three review units, each unit is made up of three or four sections. The beginning of each section will remind you of your objective and introduce you briefly, in English, to the theme of the section. Read these introductions carefully—they'll give you pieces of information about German-speaking people and their way of life.

SECTION D — asking and telling where you are from

Now you will meet some young people from the German-speaking countries.

D1 Woher bist du?

Ich heisse Jens Kröger. Ich bin sechzehn Jahre alt. Ich bin aus Niebüll, aus Deutschland.

Jens Kröger, 16
Niebüll, Deutschland

Ich bin die Wiebke Nedel. Ich bin fünfzehn. Ich bin auch aus Deutschland, aus Neuss.

Wiebke Nedel, 15
Neuss, Deutschland

Ich heisse Dastl, Margit Dastl. Ich bin vierzehn. Ich bin aus Wien, aus Österreich.

Margit Dastl, 14
Wien, Österreich

Ich heisse Bruno Schmidlin. Ich bin auch fünfzehn. Ich bin aus der Schweiz, aus Zimmerwald.

Bruno Schmidlin, 15
Zimmerwald, Schweiz

Ich bin Kurt Langer. Ich bin 15. Ich bin aus der DDR, aus Dresden.

Kurt Langer, 15
Dresden, DDR

Und woher bist du? Aus Kansas City? Aus Harrisburg? Aus Dallas? Ich bin aus _____.

Neue Freunde   45

C7 WIE SAGT MAN DAS?
Asking someone's age and telling yours

QUESTION	ANSWER
Wie alt bist du? *How old are you?*	Ich bin dreizehn Jahre alt. *I'm thirteen years old.*
Wie alt ist der Stefan? *How old is Stefan?*	Er ist fünfzehn. *He is fifteen.*
Wie alt ist die Sabine? *How old is Sabine?*	Sie ist fünfzehn Jahre alt. *She's fifteen years old.*
Wie alt sind Ulrike und Jochen? *How old are Ulrike and Jochen?*	Sie sind auch fünfzehn. *They are also fifteen.*

COMMUNICATIVE FUNCTIONS

The material labeled **Wie sagt man das?** *(How do you say that?)* summarizes the sentences, phrases, and expressions you'll need in order to accomplish your purpose—that is, to express and react to requests, opinions, and emotions. Mastery of this material is the key to meeting the objective or objectives of the section.

C8 ERKLÄRUNG *Explanation*
Personal Pronouns and the Verb sein

The phrases **ich bin, du bist, er ist, sie ist,** and **sie sind** each contain a subject pronoun corresponding to the English *I, you, he, she,* and *they*, plus a form of the verb **sein,** *to be: I am, you are, he/she/it is, they are.* **Sein** is one of the most frequently used verbs in German. The chart shows the plural forms **wir,** *we,* and **ihr,** *you* (plural), but you do not need to use them yet.

Singular			Plural		
Ich	bin		Wir	sind	
Du	bist		Ihr	seid	
Der Stefan / Er	ist	15 Jahre alt.	Stefan and Sabine / Sie	sind	15 Jahre alt.
Die Sabine / Sie	ist				

GRAMMAR

In order to communicate effectively, you'll need to understand and use some grammatical forms. Look for these forms in the boxes with the heading **Erklärung** *(Explanation)*. Once again, the color blue is a cue that the material in the box is to be mastered.

C9 Übung • Wie alt sind die Schüler? —Vierzehn.

Everyone in this group is 14 years old.

A: Wie alt ist der Fritz?
B: Er ist vierzehn.

1. Wie alt ist der Hans?
2. Wie alt ist die Monika?
3. Wie alt sind Hans und Monika?
4. Wie alt ist der Günter?
5. Wie alt ist die Ulrike?
6. Wie alt sind Günter and Ulrike?

Neue Freunde   43

BASIC MATERIAL

The material in each section is numbered in sequence together with the letter of the section: A1, A2, A3, and so on. The first presentation is always new or basic material, signaled by a number and title in blue. In some sections new material may be introduced in two or three other places. Whenever you see a heading in blue, you'll know that there's something new to learn. The new material is a model of what to say in a situation. Its authentic language and pictures will acquaint you with the way German-speaking people live, think, and feel and familiarize you with the various settings in which German is spoken.

ACTIVITIES

The headings of all the activities in the section begin with the word **Übung** in orange. This signals an opportunity to practice and work with new material—and sometimes old material—either orally or in writing. Many of the activities are designed so that you may work together with your classmates in pairs or in small groups.

LISTENING

Listening is an essential skill that requires practice to develop. Whenever you see this cassette symbol ▤ after a heading, you'll know that the material is recorded, with pauses provided for your repetition or responses. A special listening comprehension activity in each section is headed **Hör gut zu!** *(Listen carefully).* In order to respond, you will need to listen as your teacher plays the cassette or reads the German to you.

CULTURE NOTES

The head **Ein wenig Landeskunde** *(A little culture)* printed in green invites you to find out more about the life of German-speaking people. These culture notes in English provide additional information about the theme of the section to help you increase your cultural awareness.

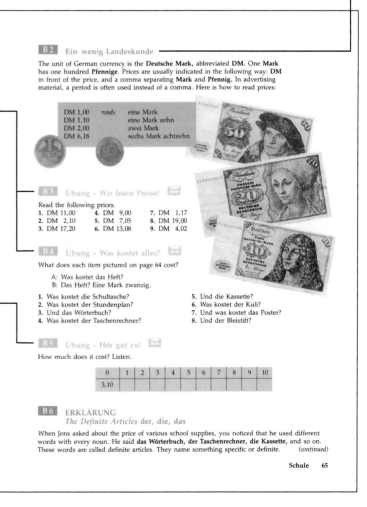

B2 Ein wenig Landeskunde

The unit of German currency is the **Deutsche Mark**, abbreviated **DM.** One **Mark** has one hundred **Pfennige**. Prices are usually indicated in the following way: **DM** in front of the price, and a comma separating **Mark** and **Pfennig**. In advertising material, a period is often used instead of a comma. Here is how to read prices:

DM 1,00	*reads*	eine Mark
DM 1,10		eine Mark zehn
DM 2,00		zwei Mark
DM 6,18		sechs Mark achtzehn

B3 Übung · Wir lesen Preise!

Read the following prices.
1. DM 11,00   4. DM 9,00   7. DM 1,17
2. DM 2,10   5. DM 7,05   8. DM 19,00
3. DM 17,20   6. DM 13,08   9. DM 4,02

B4 Übung · Was kostet alles?

What does each item pictured on page 64 cost?

A: Was kostet das Heft?
B: Das Heft? Eine Mark zwanzig.

1. Was kostet die Schultasche?
2. Was kostet der Stundenplan?
3. Und das Wörterbuch?
4. Was kostet der Taschenrechner?
5. Und die Kassette?
6. Was kostet der Kuli?
7. Und was kostet das Poster?
8. Und der Bleistift?

B5 Übung · Hör gut zu!

How much does it cost? Listen.

	0	1	2	3	4	5	6	7	8	9	10
3,10											

B6 ERKLÄRUNG
The Definite Articles der, die, das

When Jens asked about the price of various school supplies, you noticed that he used different words with every noun. He said **das Wörterbuch, der Taschenrechner, die Kassette**, and so on. These words are called definite articles. They name something specific or definite.   *(continued)*

Schule   65

TRY YOUR SKILLS

This section will let you experiment with the skills and knowledge you've gathered in the previous sections of the unit. Its variety of activities will give you many opportunities to practice communicating with others.

1   Gerd Ecker in den USA

Gerd Ecker, a student from Germany, introduces himself to your class.

Guten Tag! Ich heisse Gerd Ecker. Ich bin 16 Jahre alt. Ich bin aus Paderborn. Paderborn ist in der Bundesrepublik Deutschland. Ich gehe aufs Goerdeler Gymnasium. Ich komme mit dem Rad in die Schule, und die Klassenkameraden—ja, sie kommen mit dem Bus, mit dem Moped, mit dem Auto und auch zu Fuss.
   Wir haben von Montag bis Freitag Schule. Wir haben Sonnabend frei. Die Schule beginnt um Viertel vor acht, und sie ist um ein Uhr aus.
   Welche Fächer ich habe? Nun, ich habe Deutsch, Mathe, Englisch, Geschichte, Geographie, Sport und Kunst. Ich bin gut in Englisch und in Deutsch. Ich habe eine Eins in Englisch und eine Zwei in Deutsch. Englisch und Deutsch sind leicht. Ich bin nicht so gut in Mathe. Mathe ist schwer. Ich habe nur eine Vier.

2   Übung • Rollenspiel

A classmate plays the role of Gerd. You missed some of his presentation, so you ask him questions about himself. Then you take the role of Gerd, and your classmate asks you.

   A: Wie heisst du?
   B: Ich heisse. . .

3   Übung • Erzähl mal, was Gerd gesagt hat!

A friend of yours missed Gerd's presentation. You tell him or her what Gerd said.

   Der Schüler aus Deutschland heisst. . .

4   Übung • Vortrag   *Presentation*

You are visiting a class in Germany. Tell the class something about yourself and your school day.

WAS KANNST DU SCHON?

Let's review some important points that you have learned in this unit.

SECTION A

Can you greet young people and adults in German?
Say hello to the following people:

   1. Katrin   3. Mr. Sperling   5. Mrs. Meier
   2. Stefan   4. Miss Seifert   6. your teacher

Can you say goodbye in German?
Say goodbye to the same people.

SECTION B

Can you introduce yourself in German?
   1. Say hello.   3. Ask a classmate his or her
   2. Give your name.   name.

Can you find out who someone is?
   1. Ask a boy's name, then tell it to someone else.
   2. Ask a girl's name, then tell it to someone else.
   3. Ask who someone is and give the answer.

SECTION C

Can you ask someone's age and tell yours?
Write a question and answer about age for each of the following pronouns:
   ich, du, er, sie, sie (plural).

Do you know the numbers from 0 to 20?
Write out in German the numbers from 0 to 20.

Do you know the forms of the verb *sein*?
Complete the following sentences.
   1. Das Mädchen _____ 15.   5. _____ du aus Deutschland?
   2. Ich _____ 13.   6. Wer _____ das?
   3. Der Junge _____ 16.   7. Jens und Wiebke _____ aus Deutschland.
   4. Frl. Seifert _____ aus Wien. 8. Er _____ aus Österreich.

SECTION D

Can you say where you are from? Can you ask where others are from?
Say where you are from. Ask one of your classmates where he or she is from.

Can you ask questions anticipating a yes or no answer?
Make up three questions anticipating a yes or no answer.

Can you ask for information to be repeated?
What do you say if you don't understand part or all of the following statements?
   1. Ich bin aus Deutschland.   3. Das Mädchen ist 15 Jahre alt.
   2. Er heisst Jens Kröger.   4. Der Deutschlehrer heisst Sperling.

Can you address adults using the *Sie*-form?
Ask your teacher his or her name and where he or she is from.

SELF-CHECK

Each of the nine basic units ends with a one-page self-check called **Was kannst du schon?** *(What have you learned?)*. It includes a series of questions in English for you to ask yourself. Following the questions are short activities that will check your knowledge and skills. The questions and activities are grouped by section, so if you can't answer yes to a question or if the exercise shows that you need to review, you'll know which section to turn to.

WORTSCHATZ

SECTION A

armer Peter! *poor Peter!*
bei den Nedels *at the Nedels'*
der Bruder, ⁻ *brother*
da: wir sind da *we're here*
das sind *these are*
dass *that*
die Freundin, -nen *girl friend*
die Geschwister (pl) *brothers and sisters*
die Grosseltern (pl) *grandparents*
der Hund, -e *dog*
kennenlernen: du lernst viele Leute kennen *you're going to meet a lot of people*
die Klassenkameradin, -nen *classmate (f)*
die Kusine, -n *cousin (f)*
die Leute (pl) *people*
mein, meine *my*
die Oma, -s *grandma*
der Onkel, - *uncle*
der Opa, -s *grandpa*
schlimm *bad*
schön *nice; schön, dass du da bist nice that you're here*
die Schwester, -n *sister*
so *so, well then*
die Tante, -n *aunt*
der Vetter, -n *cousin (m)*
viele *many*
von *of; ein Freund von Wiebke a friend of Wiebke's*
Willkommen in Neuss! *welcome to Neuss!*

SECTION B

der Audi, -s *Audi (a German-made automobile)*
auf *on*
auspacken: er packt den

Rucksack aus *he unpacks his backpack*
aussehen *to look (like), appear, (see p 179)*
das Auto, -s *car*
das Bad, ⁻er *bathroom*
bekommen *to get, receive*
bitte schön *you're welcome*
das Buch, ⁻er *book*
Dank: vielen Dank! *thanks a lot! tausend Dank! thanks a million!*
danken *to thank; nichts zu danken don't mention it*
dein, deine *your*
das Esszimmer, - *dining room*
finden: findest du? *do you think so?*
die Garage, -n *garage*
der Garten, ⁻ *garden*
das Gästezimmer, - *guest room*
gemütlich *cozy, comfortable*
gern: ja, gern *yes, I'd like that*
gross *big*
die Halskette, -n *necklace*
das Haus, ⁻er *house*
hell *light*
der Keller, - *basement, cellar*
klein *small*
komm! *come on!*
die Küche, -n *kitchen*
mehr *more*
Mensch! *boy! wow!*
modern *modern*
oben *upstairs*
die Party, -s *party*
der Rucksack, ⁻e *knapsack, backpack*
das Schlafzimmer, - *bedroom*
schön *pretty, beautiful*
sehen *to see*
sehr *very*
stehen: da steht noch mehr auf Peters Zettel *there's still*

more on Peter's slip
tausend *thousand; tausend Dank! thanks a million!*
die Toilette, -n *toilet*
unten *downstairs*
wieviel? *how many?*
das Wohnzimmer, - *living room*
zeigen *to show; ich zeig es dir I'll show it to you*
der Zettel, - *note, slip of paper*
das Zimmer, - *room*

SECTION C

arrogant *arrogant*
attraktiv *attractive*
aussehen: gut aussehen *to look good; to be handsome, pretty, attractive*
blond *blond*
die Brille, -n *glasses*
brünett *brunette*
dunkel *dark*
dunkelblond *dark blond*
freundlich *friendly*
Geschmackssache: das ist Geschmackssache *that's a matter of taste*
gross *tall*
hübsch *pretty*
kennen *to know*
klein *short, small*
lustig *merry, funny*
meinen: meinst du? *do you think so? meinst du nicht? don't you think so?*
nett *nice*
nicht? *don't you thin[k]*
recht haben *to be ri[ght]*
schlank *slim*
sympathisch *likeable*
unsympathisch *un[pleasant?] not nice*
vollschlank *heavyse[t]*

WORTSCHATZÜBUNGEN

1. Look at the Wortschatz and make a list of all singular nouns with their definite articles. Then write the nouns again with their indefinite articles.

2. Pick out all the adjectives and write them down. How many pairs of opposites can you find? Write them next to each other.

Bei den Nede[ls]

VOCABULARY

The German-English vocabulary list **(Wortschatz)** after the self-check contains the unit words and phrases you'll need to know. They're grouped according to the sections of the unit. A word-study exercise, **Wortschatzübung,** below the list will focus your attention on various aspects of the vocabulary and provide helpful ways to work with and learn the new words and phrases.

READING

A reading section, **Zum Lesen** (*To Read*), concludes the unit. Here you'll find one or more reading selections related to the unit's theme. They include comic strips, postcards, interviews, opinion polls of German teenagers, factual selections, and stories. Most reading selections are followed by questions and activities designed to help you practice and develop your reading skills.

ZUM LESEN
Ein Gewohnheitsmensch

Herr Neuschuh ist ein netter Mann. Er ist höflich°, pünktlich, immer korrekt. Er ist auch immer gut angezogen°: er kauft seine Sachen in den besten Geschäften°. Aber er macht sich wenig aus der Mode°. „Die Mode", so sagt er, „ist nur für die Jugend." Herr Neuschuh liebt den klassischen Stil. Seine Anzüge° kommen aus England, seine Krawatten kommen aus Frankreich und seine Schuhe aus Italien. Jeden Morgen, bevor Herr Neuschuh zur Arbeit geht, bürstet er seinen Anzug und putzt° seine Schuhe. Er ist ein schicker Herr°.

Nun, eines Tages möchte Herr Neuschuh ein Paar neue Schuhe. Er geht in das Schuhgeschäft, wo er immer seine Schuhe kauft. Dort kennt er alle Verkäufer.
„Guten Tag, Herr Neuschuh! Was darf es heute sein?"
„Ist Frl. Seidel nicht da?"
„Frl. Seidel ist gestern in Urlaub gegangen°."
„Ach, so was! —Nun, das macht nichts°. Ich möchte ein Paar Schuhe."
„Welche Marke°?"
„Diese hier."

ein Gewohnheitsmensch *a creature of habit;* höflich *polite;* gut angezogen *well-dressed;* das Geschäft *store;* er macht sich wenig aus der Mode *he doesn't pay much attention to fashion, to what's in style;* der Anzug *suit;* putzen *to clean, polish;* ein schicker Herr *a smartly-dressed gentleman;* in Urlaub gehen *to go on vacation;* das macht nichts *it doesn't matter;* die Marke *make*

324   Kapitel 11

PHOTO ESSAYS

Following each of the three review units in the textbook, you'll find a cultural photo essay called **Landeskunde.** The three essays tell you more about the lives of the German-speaking people and the places where they live.

LANDESKUNDE 1

A Glimpse of the Federal Republic of Germany

Germany lies in the center of Europe. It is about six hundred miles long, bounded by the North Sea to the north and the Alps to the south. From east to west the country is narrow, seldom more than two hundred miles wide. Contained in this area is a surprising variety of landscapes. There are coastal regions and flatlands in northern Germany and gently rolling hills in the central and southwestern part of the country. South of the river Danube is a high plateau that reaches to the majestic Alpine range. It is surprising that in such a highly industrialized country more than half the area is farmland and another third is forest land.

❶ Promenadenkonzert auf der Nordseeinsel Sylt

❷ Kurort Badenweiler im Schwarzwald

❸ Die Zugspitze, Deutschlands höchster Berg, 2 963 m

125

LANDESKUNDE 2

Other German-speaking Countries and Regions

The German Democratic Republic

The German Democratic Republic (GDR) is located in Central Europe, with the Federal Republic to the west, Poland to the east, and Czechoslovakia to the south. The GDR is a socialist state, formed in 1949 from the Soviet-occupied zone of Germany, six months after the formation of the Federal Republic. In the GDR all decision making is in the hands of the communist party, officially known as the Socialist

Unity Party (SED). Geographically, the northern and central parts of the GDR are a low-lying plain intersected by gentle ranges of hills. The southern part of the country is highland. Some of the chief cities are (East) Berlin, the capital; Leipzig, a center of printing and book trade and the site of trade fairs since 1100; Dresden, a baroque art city that has been carefully restored; and the port of Rostock on the Baltic Sea.

Die Deutsche Demokratische Republik feiert ihren 35. Geburtstag

LANDESKUNDE 3

Festivals and Holidays

It is said that in Germany festivals are as numerous as the days of the year. This is no exaggeration! Wherever you go, there is always something going on—a popular festival, a religious feast, a folk-dance, a historical or costume parade, or simply some occasion for public merrymaking. The calendar of festivities begins with carnival, a season that starts on the seventh of January and lasts until Lent, 40 days before Easter. It is celebrated mostly in the Catholic areas. The Rhenish carnival turns Cologne, Düsseldorf, and Mainz "upside down." During the famous "Fasching," its Bavarian counterpart, Munich celebrates. The Swabian "Fasnet" conjures up the ghosts and demons of old in the strange dance of bell-jingling masks.

❶ Fastnacht in Rottweil, Schwaben

❷ Lustige Maske

❸ Rosenmontag in Köln; keiner arbeitet, alle feiern Karneval auf der Strasse

❹ Kinderfasching

333

SUMMARY OF FUNCTIONS

The term *functions* can be defined as what you do with language—what your purpose is in speaking. As you use this textbook, you will find yourself in a number of situations—in a store, in a restaurant, at a party, at the airport, in a new city. How do you "function" in these situations? How do you ask about prices in a store, order a meal in a restaurant, compliment your host at a party, greet arriving friends at an airport, or ask for directions in an unfamiliar city? You need to know certain basic functional expressions.

Here is a list of functions accompanied by the expressions you have learned to communicate them. The number of the unit in which the expressions were introduced is followed by the section letter and number in parentheses.

SOCIALIZING

Saying hello
1 (A3)   Guten Morgen!
         Guten Tag!
         short forms: Morgen!
                        Tag!
         informal: Hallo!
         regional: Grüss dich!
7 (A1)   Grüss Gott!
         Gruetzi!

Saying goodbye
1 (A3)   Auf Wiedersehen!
         short form: Wiedersehen!
         informal: Tschüs!
                     Tschau!
                     Bis dann!
5 (C6)   Bis gleich!

Addressing people
1 (A1)   *first name*
1 (A7)   Herr + *last name*
         Frau + *last name*

Responding to an introduction
6 (A3)   Guten Tag, + *name*
         Hallo, + *first name*
         Grüss dich, + *first name*. Wie geht's?

Asking "How are you?"
10 (A9) Wie geht's?
         Wie geht's denn?

Responding to "How are you?"
10 (A9) Ach, prima!
         Danke, gut!
         Nicht schlecht.
         So lala.
         Schlecht.
         Miserabel.

Welcoming people
6 (A1)   Willkommen in . . . !
         Schön, dass du hier bist!

Getting someone's attention
2 (B25) Du, (Jens), . . .
         Schau!
         Schau, (Jens)!

GRAMMAR SUMMARY

DETERMINERS

In German, nouns can be grouped into three classes or genders: masculine, feminine, and neuter. There are words that tell you the gender of a noun. One of these is called the definite article. In English there is one definite article: *the*. In German there are three, one for each gender: **der**, **die**, and **das**.

Gender:	MASCULINE	FEMININE	NEUTER
Noun Phrase:	**der Junge** *the boy* **der Ball** *the ball*	**die Mutter** *the mother* **die Kassette** *the cassette*	**das Mädchen** *the girl* **das Haus** *the house*

Other words can be used with a noun instead of the definite article. Examples of these words in English are *a, this, that, my,* and *every*. These words and the definite article are called determiners. They help to make clear, or determine, which person or thing you mean—for example, whether you are talking about *this book, my book,* or just any book. A determiner plus a noun is called a noun phrase.

GERMAN-ENGLISH VOCABULARY

This vocabulary includes almost all words in this textbook, both active and passive. Active words and phrases are those introduced in basic material and listed in the **Wortschatz** sections of the units. You are expected to know and be able to use active vocabulary. All other words—those appearing in the Introduction, in exercises, in optional and visual material, in the Try Your Skills and **Zum Lesen** sections, in the review units, and in the pictorial **Landeskunde** sections—are considered passive. Passive vocabulary is for recognition only. The meaning of passive words and phrases can usually be understood from context or may be looked up in this vocabulary.

With some exceptions, the following are not included: most proper nouns, forms of verbs other than the infinitive, and forms of determiners other than the nominative.

Nouns are listed with definite article and plural form, when applicable. The numbers in the entries refer to the unit where the word or phrase first appears. A number in black, heavy type indicates that the word or phrase has been actively introduced in that unit. Passive vocabulary is followed by numerals in light type.

The following abbreviations are used in this vocabulary: adj (adjective), pl (plural), pp (past participle), sep (separable prefix), sing (singular), and s. th. (something).

A

ab *from, starting at, 4; leaves,*

FOR REFERENCE

The reference section at the end of the textbook provides you with valuable aids. It is grouped into the following parts: Summary of Functions, Grammar Summary, Pronunciation, Numbers, English Equivalents, German-English Vocabulary, English-German Vocabulary, and Grammar Index.

SUMMARY OF FUNCTIONS

The Summary of Functions sums up the communicative functions you have learned and practiced in a variety of situations throughout this textbook. If you want to ask for directions, invite someone to a party, pay a compliment, or respond to a friend's good fortune, for example, you will find the appropriate phrases and sentences listed here, as well as the unit in which the particular function was introduced.

GRAMMAR SUMMARY

The grammar points that have been presented in the textbook are organized in tables for easy reference and review in the Grammar Summary.

GERMAN-ENGLISH VOCABULARY

The German-English Vocabulary includes almost all the words you will come across in this textbook. The numbers after each entry tell you in which unit the word first appeared. If the number is in heavy type, you are expected to know that word or phrase and be able to use it. In this Vocabulary, you can look up the English meanings of words and phrases, and you can check the gender of nouns as well as the plural forms.

BITTE SCHÖN!

There it is, a special textbook that will help you enlarge your view of the world and enable you to contribute to better understanding and communication among people. Now you're ready to begin an exciting, rewarding experience— learning another language and meeting new friends, **Neue Freunde.**

INTRODUCTION

German and You

Welcome to the German-speaking world! During the coming year you will learn to understand, speak, read, and write German in a variety of situations. You will also learn more about the German-speaking world outside your classroom: daily life, customs, traditions, music, art, science, and history. As you begin your travels through the German-speaking world, here's wishing you . . .

Viel Glück!
Good luck!

In this introduction you will learn about:

 1   Germany: a pictorial view

 2   the German-speaking countries

 3   German in the United States

 4   German, English, and other languages

 5   German and your future career

 6   suggestions for studying German

What comes to mind when you think of Germany? Majestic castles along the Rhine? Quaint medieval villages? Fairy tales? The Black Forest? The Alps? Bavarian folk costume? Fast, elegant cars? Scientists? Modern technology? Beethoven? Goethe? Einstein?

Germany is all of these things—some of them just as you imagined, others quite different. But Germany is also images you may not have pictured. The following pages take you on an armchair tour of Germany. It's not the same as being there, of course, but see how these glimpses compare with your image of Germany.

Germany is a land of abundance . . .

and a land of contrasts—mountains and flatlands,

forests and farmlands,

seaports and overland routes.

The country is strongly regional

and busily cosmopolitan,

highly industrialized

and artistically individual.

There are ordinary stores for everyday things

and elegant stores for luxuries.

Germany is rich in tradition . . .

and rich in innovation.

In Germany, history is
a part of everyday life and
can be traced through its existing
architecture, which is not only
still standing but often
still in use.

Germany has elegant restaurants . . .

and cozy inns;

exciting theater, music, and art . . . both indoors

and outdoors.

And from Germany have come great composers,

J. S. Bach (1685–1750)   Beethoven (1770–1827)

great artists,

Kokoschka (1886–1980)

Dürer (1471–1528)

great poets and writers,

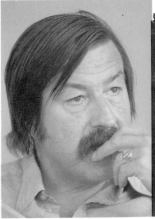

Hesse (1877–1963)   Grass (1927–   )   Goethe (1749–1832)

great philosophers,

Kant (1724–1804)

Nietzsche (1844–1900)

great inventors,

Daimler (1834–1900)

Gutenberg (before 1400–1468)

great scientists,

Mössbauer (1929)

Einstein (1879–1955)

12   Introduction

great filmmakers

von Trotta   Herzog

as well as great stars.

Brandauer

Dietrich

Schygulla

German is the native language of more than 100 million people in Austria, East and West Germany, Liechtenstein, Switzerland, and parts of France and Italy. It is used as a second language by many others in Central Europe.

For a map of the German-speaking countries turn to page 57.

Bundesrepublik Deutschland

Area: 96,010 sq. mi.
Population: 60.7 million
Monetary unit:
   Deutsche Mark
Capital: Bonn

The area of Central Europe historically regarded as Germany was split into two zones of occupation after World War II. The western part of Germany was occupied by Britain, France, and the United States and is known today as the Federal Republic of Germany.

Deutsche Demokratische Republik

Area: 41,767 sq. mi.
Population: 16.7 million
Monetary unit:
   Mark of the Deutsche
   Demokratische Republik
Capital: Berlin (Ost)

The eastern part of Germany was occupied by the Soviet Union after World War II and is known today as the German Democratic Republic. The prewar capital of Germany—Berlin—was also divided into occupation zones after the war. East Berlin is now the capital of the German Democratic Republic; West Berlin is a part of the Federal Republic.

Österreich

Area: 32,375 sq. mi.
Population: 7.6 million
Monetary unit:
  Schilling
Capital: Vienna

Austria is just a little larger than the state of South Carolina. Its beautiful mountain scenery, art, and music attract millions of tourists each year. One fifth of the population of Austria lives in the capital city of Vienna.

Schweiz / Suisse / Svizzera

Area: 15,941 sq. mi.
Population: 6.5 million
Monetary unit:
  Swiss franc
Capital: Bern

Switzerland is the land of the Alps, famous for its spectacular scenery, luxurious ski resorts, and, of course, Swiss cheese. Switzerland has three official languages: French, Italian, and German. Seventy percent of the population speaks Swiss German or **Schwyzerdütsch.** A fourth language, spoken by about 1 percent of the total population, is called Romansh. It is closely related to Latin and is spoken only in the canton of Graubünden.

Liechtenstein

Area: 61 sq. mi.
Population: 28,000
Monetary unit:
  Swiss franc
Capital: Vaduz

Liechtenstein is one of the smallest countries in the world. Its area is less than that of Washington, D.C. Nestled between Germany, Austria, and Switzerland, the principality of Liechtenstein has close ties with Switzerland. The two countries share similar customs. Swiss currency is used in Liechtenstein, and Switzerland operates Liechtenstein's postal, telegraph, and telephone systems. Switzerland also represents Liechtenstein in diplomatic and trade relations.

Can you guess how many Americans trace all or part of their ethnic background to the countries of Germany, Austria, or Switzerland?—5 million? 15 million? 25 million? 50 million? If you guessed 50 million, you are right! According to a recent survey published by the U.S. Census Bureau, 52 million people or 28.8 percent of the total population reported that they were at least partly of German ancestry.

Germans were among the earliest settlers in the United States. On October 6, 1683, a group arrived from Krefeld, Germany, on the *Concord*, a ship that has since been nicknamed the "German Mayflower." They settled in Pennsylvania and founded Germantown. These early settlers quickly established their own schools, print shops, and newspapers. It was a small German newspaper that gave the first report of the Declaration of Independence on July 5, 1776. In fact, German almost became the official language of the United States. The Continental Congress at one point thought of having a new language for this country, and German was considered a good choice for a number of reasons. When it came to a vote, however, English was chosen instead of German by the slim majority of one vote!

Since 1683 more than seven million immigrants from German-speaking regions of Europe have come to the shores of North America. These immigrants influenced the history and development of this country and over the years have made many contributions.

In many parts of the country there are reminders of the role Germans have played in the development of the United States. You can find names of towns and cities such as Hanover, Berlin, and Potsdam. Steubenville, Ohio, was named in honor of Friedrich Wilhelm von Steuben, the German officer who trained George Washington's army. The state where you live may have place names that are German in origin and would be interesting to research.

Baron von Steuben inspecting
the squalid conditions at Valley Forge

The trial of John Peter Zenger in New York in 1735. The printer of the *New York Weekly Journal* was accused of criminal libel. He was acquitted, and this precedent established freedom of the press in this country.

German family names are also plentiful in the United States. There are last names such as Klein, Myer (or Meyer, Maier, Meier), and Schneider. Very often German family names indicate occupations (Bauer, *farmer*), places (Berlin or Berliner, *a citizen of Berlin*), or physical descriptions (Kraft, *strong*). If you are interested in tracing the origins of German family names, keep in mind that there may have been changes—for example, Schmidt may have become Smith; Mueller may have turned into Miller.

Many words and phrases contributed by the German immigrants have become part of our everyday language—pumpernickel, noodle, hausfrau, lager beer and bock beer, wienerwurst (often shortened to wiener or wienie), sauerbraten, schnitzel, dachshund, zwieback, delicatessen, kindergarten, and katzenjammer. And don't forget those ''typically American'' foods such as hamburgers, pretzels, liverwurst, and frankfurters with sauerkraut—all introduced by the Germans.

The Germans who came to the United States brought customs that have become part of our way of life. They introduced the Christmas tree (as well as many Christmas carols), the Easter bunny and Easter egg hunts, county fairs, and more recently, the folk march or Volksmarsch, which has made its appearance in many communities.

And there is a long list of individual Germans who have made invaluable contributions to this country in art and music, science and

Peter Lorre

John Jacob Astor

Levi Strauss

industry, education and politics. From John Peter Zenger to Levi Strauss, from Albert Einstein to Marlene Dietrich, German names appear throughout our history.

Activities

1. See how many German names you and your classmates can find in your local telephone book.
2. Get a map of your state and circle any German place names.
3. Visit your local historical society. Find out about any Germans who may have settled in your area. Historical societies often have documents, correspondence, and sometimes even pictures and memoirs of early settlers.
4. Choose a famous German-American to research in the library and give a short report to the class. As a class project, make a bulletin board display of famous German-Americans. Here are a few suggestions: John Peter Zenger, Friedrich Wilhelm von Steuben, John Jacob Astor, Carl Schurz, Levi Strauss, Leopold Damrosch, Maximilian Berlitz, Charles Steinmetz, Albert Einstein, Mies van der Rohe, Hannah Arendt, Wernher von Braun, Henry Kissinger.
5. As you study German this year, be aware of news about German-speaking countries. You may hear of visits by well-known Germans to the United States. Also, news about sports events, athletes, films, or new German cars may interest you. Keep track of current events in German-speaking countries. Keep a scrapbook with articles and information you find.

Kristin ist 14 Jahre alt.

As you look at this German sentence, you may be able to guess its meaning because some words remind you of English. If you guessed "Kristin is fourteen years old," you are right. The verb *ist* is close to the English *is.* If you pronounce *Jahre,* it sounds something like the English *year,* and the German *alt* seems to be related to *old* in some way or other. The explanation for these similarities is that German and English belong to the same family tree. They are both Germanic languages, tracing their roots back to Germanic languages that began to appear in written form as early as the first century B.C.

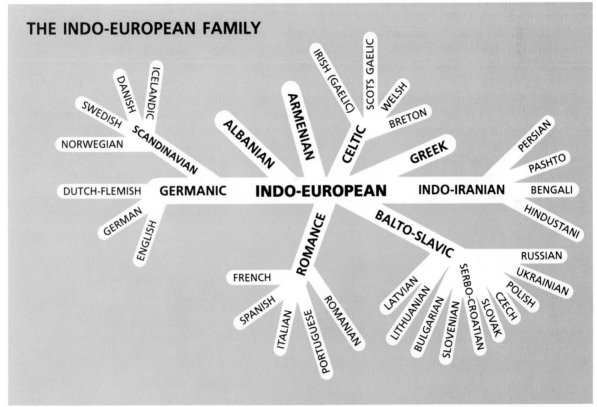

THE INDO-EUROPEAN FAMILY

About half the words in English are Germanic in origin. They are basic words in such categories as family, food, farming, parts of the body, and everyday living. See if you can guess the meaning of these German words: Vater, Mutter, Bruder, Milch, Apfel, Finger, Fuss, Hand. Easy! These look-alikes are called *cognates* and may help you particularly when you read German. But be careful of false cognates— words that look like English words but have totally different meanings. A **Teller** in German is a plate and not someone who works in a bank. **Gift** means poison in German, not a present!

The Indo-European language family is divided into several groups, such as Germanic, Romance, and Balto-Slavic. About half of the people in the world speak a language belonging to this family.

German and English are also related to Dutch and to the Dutch-related languages of Flemish and Afrikaans, and also to Danish and the related languages of Norwegian and Swedish. They are all Germanic languages and have many words in common. Compare the following examples:

English	German	Dutch	Danish
bath	Bad	bad	bad
blind	blind	blind	blind
book	Buch	boek	bog
father	Vater	vader	fader
think	denken	denken	taenke

As you compare these words, you will notice something interesting. Look at the English words *bath*, *father*, and *think* and at the German words *Bad*, *Vater*, and *denken*. Of all the North Germanic languages, English and Icelandic are the only ones to have retained the *th* sound of the old Anglo-Saxon letter thorn, þ. In the course of time the *th* sound changed to *d* or *t* in the other Germanic languages, including German.

In your study of German, use what you know about English and other languages. You have learned about cognates and have seen that many words in German and English are the same or similar. You will find that many English words have been incorporated into German: der Boss, der Manager, der Job, der Computer, die Jeans, das Sweatshirt, das T-shirt, das Baby, der Teenager.

The alphabet used in German is also the same as the one used in English, although the names of the letters are pronounced differently. Here is how German-speakers say the alphabet:

German Letters		Roman Letters		German Name	German Letters		Roman Letters		German Name
𝔄	a	A	a	[ah]	𝔑	n	N	n	[en]
𝔅	b	B	b	[bay]	𝔒	o	O	o	[oh]
ℭ	c	C	c	[tsay]	𝔓	p	P	p	[pay]
𝔇	d	D	d	[day]	𝔔	q	Q	q	[koo]
𝔈	e	E	e	[ay]	ℜ	r	R	r	[air]
𝔉	f	F	f	[ef]	𝔖	s	S	s	[ess]
𝔊	g	G	g	[gay]	𝔗	t	T	t	[tay]
ℌ	h	H	h	[hah]	𝔘	u	U	u	[oo]
ℑ	i	I	i	[ee]	𝔙	v	V	v	[fow]
𝔍	j	J	j	[yot]	𝔚	w	W	w	[vay]
𝔎	k	K	k	[kah]	𝔛	x	X	x	[iks]
𝔏	l	L	l	[el]	𝔜	y	Y	y	[ipsilon]
𝔐	m	M	m	[em]	ℨ	ʒ	Z	z	[tset]

As in English, German words can be grouped into word families. Look at the example below. Knowing the key word **Zimmer,** *room,* helps you to remember or to figure out the meaning of other words in the family.

Zimmer *room*	Badezimmer *bathroom*
Wohnzimmer *living room*	im Nebenzimmer *in the next room*
Schlafzimmer *bedroom*	Zimmerpflanze *house plant*
Arbeitszimmer *workroom*	

You will find other similarities between German and English, and you will also find differences. You have probably noticed that all nouns in German are capitalized. You will discover that there are many more endings to verbs, articles, and adjectives in German than there are in English. And word order in German sentences can be quite different. If you try to render a German sentence word for word in English, the results would be quite amusing! As you learn more German, you will become aware of other differences. Comparing these differences with English will help you to understand how both languages operate.

Activities

1. Can you spell aloud—in German—these common acronyms and abbreviations that are used in Germany?

   1. BMW   3. dtv   5. BRD   7. USA
   2. VW   4. ADAC   6. DDR   8. GmbH

2. Here is a list, in German, of items you can find at home or at school. See how many you can identify just by guessing. You can check your answers in the German-English Vocabulary at the back of this textbook.

1. die Lampe	6. die Tomate	11. die Schokolade
2. das Poster	7. der Joghurt	12. die Milch
3. das Sofa	8. das Telefon	13. die Waschmaschine
4. die Banane	9. das Mathematikbuch	14. der Fotoapparat
5. die Butter	10. das Papier	15. der Kassetten-Recorder

3. Pennsylvania Dutch (Dutch = Deutsch, *German*) is still spoken in the state of Pennsylvania. How it got there in the first place is an interesting story. Track down the history of this German dialect and give a report to the class.

Have you ever wondered what you will be doing ten, fifteen, or even twenty years from now? Where you will be living and working? What kind of job you will have? For many jobs it is very helpful to know a foreign language such as German, and for some it is essential. Teachers of German must be fluent in the language and also know a great deal about the culture of German-speaking countries. They travel and study abroad or sometimes teach for a year in schools in Germany, Austria, or Switzerland to expand their knowledge. In addition, they must keep up with advances in educational technology such as microcomputers.

Interpreters of German, Spanish, and French translate speeches at the United Nations and at large international conferences. Interpreters must be able to think quickly in two languages.

Translators have to know not only the German language, but also the culture. Translators of literature need to study the author's background and style. Translators are also needed to prepare the subtitles or dubbing in English for German films shown in the United States.

Translators and interpreters at the United Nations are required to know at least two foreign languages.

These students are learning German in a language lab.

Most libraries have a foreign language section, and the knowledge of a foreign language can be most useful for a librarian.

Librarians find it very useful to know more than one language. And in the field of publishing, writers and editors use foreign language skills to produce teaching materials and textbooks like this one.

A knowledge of German can be an asset in many occupations and professions. Interested in a career in business? Over 25,000 companies in the United States are engaged in the export business and hire managers, shipping clerks, and specialists in export traffic. In addition, there are more than 500 large American companies based abroad: large manufacturing firms, major petroleum companies, banks, and engineering firms. These businesses employ more than 100,000 Americans overseas. German is particularly useful in technological fields. Many high-tech companies name German as the language they would prefer prospective employees to have studied.

Many German companies now have branches in the United States. They hire managers and other employees who speak German. Many American firms deal with companies in the German-speaking countries and need personnel who know German.

Buyers for large department stores and small specialty shops travel abroad to select merchandise—from clothing to fine china, from sports equipment to toys. German is needed not only to do business in the foreign country, but also to read catalogues, correspondence, and other documents.

People who work in the food industry often have to travel to foreign countries, where they sample and buy local products and are in close contact with local merchants. Chefs may train abroad. Food and travel writers visit restaurants and collect recipes.

Specialities from Germany

BRAUN

Many highly skilled professionals find foreign languages an asset. Economists sometimes deal with foreign countries. Financial experts may work in the international commodity and money markets. Lawyers and paralegals who specialize in international law or handle cases or conduct negotiations with companies in German-speaking countries must know German. Legal translators are also very much in demand.

Reporters, including sportswriters and sportscasters, can do a much better job if they can speak the language of the country where they are working and can also understand its culture.

Knowledge of a foreign language can be of great advantage on the stock exchange.

Foreign language is a must in international law.

Foreign correspondents need to know a foreign language to have first-hand knowledge about events.

Germany has many regional orchestras and opera companies, and young musicians often get experience playing and singing with them. A thorough knowledge of German and excellent pronunciation skills are essential for an opera singer who will sing roles in German.

A career with the U.S. government in the foreign service, with the diplomatic corps, or with the U.S. information services in foreign countries is an interesting way to use your foreign language ability.

Tourists from all over the world visit the United States. Travel agents, flight attendants, tour guides, salespeople in stores, desk clerks in hotels, waiters and waitresses in restaurants—anyone who deals with foreign travelers—should know more than one language.

To work in a foreign country you need to know the native language.

Opera singers sing roles in many languages.

Two foreign languages are required for international flight attendants.

Activities

1. Before you make your career choice, it is wise to talk to as many people as you can about their jobs—what they actually do, and what they like and don't like about their work. Find some people in your family, school, or neighborhood who use German in their work. Interview them, asking them to describe their jobs and to answer the following questions and others you might think of.

   1. What do you like best about your job? What do you like least about it?
   2. How do you use German in your work?
   3. How did you prepare for your job? What types of German courses did you take?
   4. Do you travel as part of your job?

   Write up the interview or record it to share with the class.

2. Who are the people listed below and why are they speaking German? Work in a group of two or three students. Think of as many reasons as you can why German would be useful in the jobs listed. Take notes on your ideas and report to the class. Write up your notes to post on the bulletin board. Write an imaginary interview with one of these people.

salesperson in a bookstore	museum director
soccer coach	radio announcer
auto mechanic	travel agent
pilot	waiter or waitress
aerospace engineer	librarian
research scientist	reporter

3. Choose an occupation that you might be interested in. Write a paragraph telling why you are interested in this particular occupation and how German might be of help to you in that field. Attach a picture of someone in that field if you can find one in a newspaper or magazine.

LISTEN

Listening is particularly important at the beginning because you have to get used to a whole new set of sounds. Sometimes you will need to listen very carefully to understand what is being said to you, so that you can answer in German.

PRACTICE

Learning German—or any foreign language—is like learning to play a musical instrument. You have to practice speaking, listening, reading, and writing in order to make progress. You already have these skills in English. Now you have to apply them to a new language. Practice a little every day. Several short periods are more effective than one long, last-minute cramming session.

VISUALIZE

Remembering German vocabulary is easier if you visualize what a sentence, phrase, or word means as you're studying or practicing it, orally or in writing. For example, if you're practicing a sentence like *Die Kinder schwimmen*, try to picture children swimming as you say the sentence to yourself several times.

CONNECT

Make use of your English connections. Find cognates or near-cognates (schwimmen, *to swim;* Garten, *garden;* Wasser, *water*) to help you understand the meaning of a sentence or paragraph that you are reading. Also, group German words into families to help you remember—for example, Freund, *friend;* Freundschaft, *friendship;* freundlich, *friendly.*

ORGANIZE

Use memory devices. Look for ways to organize the material you have to learn. Invent a system to help you remember a word or concept. Group vocabulary in meaningful segments. Put words in context and learn phrases rather than isolated words. Your teacher will help you to recognize patterns and devices that will make learning easier.

EXPAND

Use German outside class. Speak German—perhaps on the phone—with friends who are also studying the language. Find people in your family or in the neighborhood who know some German and practice with them. Talk into your cassette recorder in German. If you have a shortwave radio, try to pick up German-language broadcasts. Look at German magazines, newspapers, and books—you may not understand much at first, but it will get easier.

ENJOY

You may want to choose a new name in German. Join the German Club and make new friends. If there are any German-speaking exchange students in the area, make a point of meeting them and making them feel welcome. Above all, don't be afraid to make mistakes in German! Concentrate on getting your message across and have fun doing it.

SOME CLASSROOM PHRASES

Your teacher will be using German to give routine directions in the classroom. Here are a few phrases that you should recognize.

Hör(t) zu, bitte!	*Please listen.*
Sprich (sprecht) nach!	*Repeat after me.*
Noch mal!	*Again! Say it again!*
Antworte(t), bitte!	*Please answer.*
Steh(t) auf!	*Get up.*
Setz dich! (to one person)	*Sit down.*
Setzt euch! (to more than one person)	
Nimm (nehmt) ein Blatt Papier!	*Take out a piece of paper.*
Ruhe, bitte!	*Quiet, please.*
Pass(t) auf!	*Pay attention.*
Das ist richtig.	*That's right.*
Gut! Prima!	*Good.*

ERSTER TEIL

29

KAPITEL 1
Neue Freunde

Meeting new friends is exciting, especially when they speak another language. When you meet someone who speaks German, you need to know how to say hello and goodbye, how to find out a little about the person, and how to tell a bit about yourself. In this unit you will meet five new friends your own age from the Federal and Democratic Republics of Germany and from Austria and Switzerland.

In this unit you will:

SECTION A	say hello and say goodbye
SECTION B	ask someone's name and give your name
SECTION C	ask someone's age and tell your age; count from 1 to 20
SECTION D	ask and tell where someone is from
TRY YOUR SKILLS	use what you've learned
ZUM LESEN	read for practice and pleasure

School begins. Students meet and greet one another on their way to class. Let's hear what they're saying.

A1 Guten Tag! Auf Wiedersehen!

[1] **Tschau!** is the German spelling of the Italian **ciao**.

32   Kapitel 1

Make a name tag for yourself, with your own name or one chosen from those shown in A4. Practice saying hello and goodbye to your classmates, using the names on the tags.

A3 WIE SAGT MAN DAS? *How do you say that?*
Saying hello and goodbye

Here are some ways of saying hello and goodbye. **Guten Morgen!, Guten Tag!,** and **Auf Wiedersehen!** are standard. They can be used in almost any situation. You can also use the abbreviated forms **Morgen!, Tag!,** and **Wiedersehen!** The phrases **Hallo!, Grüss dich!, Tschüs!, Tschau!,** and **Bis dann!** are more casual.

SAYING HELLO		SAYING GOODBYE	
Guten Morgen!	Good morning!	Auf Wiedersehen!	Goodbye!
Morgen!	Morning.	Wiedersehen!	Bye!
Guten Tag!	Hello! Hi!		
Tag!			
Grüss dich!	Hi!	Tschüs!	Bye! So long!
Hallo!		Tschau!	
		Bis dann!	See you later.

A4 Ein wenig Landeskunde *A little culture*

These are popular first names of German boys and girls today.

Vornamen für Jungen	Vornamen für Mädchen
Frank Markus Jörg Mark Stefan Sven Dirk Christof Holger Andreas Michael Matthias	Antje Ulrike Monika Katja Daniele Claudia Natalie Marina Kirsten Nicole Silke Michaela

As the students enter their classrooms, they greet their teachers.

A6 Übung • Jetzt bist du dran *Now it's your turn*

Greet each of the people pictured below. Then say goodbye to each one.

| Lars | Uschi | Frl.[1] Müller | Herr Braun | Frau Binder |

---

[1] **Frl.** is the abbreviation of **Fräulein.**

A7 WIE SAGT MAN DAS? *How do you say that?*
Greeting adults

In German, you use **Herr** for *Mister (Mr.)*, **Frau** for *Mrs.*, and **Fräulein** for *Miss.*

Guten Tag, Herr Sperling!	Hello, Mr. Sperling.
Tag, Frau Meier!	Hi, Mrs. Meier.
Guten Morgen, Fräulein Seifert!	Good morning, Miss Seifert.

A8 Ein wenig Landeskunde *A little culture*

When you greet someone, you shake hands and make eye contact. When you greet adults, it's polite to also nod your head slightly.

A9 Übung · Hör gut zu! *Listen carefully*

Do you say this to a teacher or to a student? Listen.

	0	1	2	3	4	5	6	7	8	9
a male teacher										
a female teacher	✔									
a student										

A10 Übung · Jetzt bist du dran *Now it's your turn*

1. Greet your teacher.
2. Tell the class how you greet each of your teachers.

A11 Schreibübung *Writing practice*

Write how you would greet and say goodbye to the following people:

1. your friend Peter
2. your German teacher
3. your principal

Now that you know how to say hello, let's find out how you introduce yourself.

B1

Wie heisst du?

Grüss dich! Ich heisse Andreas. Und wie heisst du?

Ich heisse Natalie.

Und wie heisst du?
Ich heisse _____.

B2 Übung · Jetzt bist du dran

1. With a classmate, practice reading this short dialog aloud, filling in your own names. Then try saying the dialog without looking at the printed words.

   A: Hallo! Ich heisse _____. Und wie heisst du?
   B: Ich heisse _____.

2. Now practice with other classmates.

B3 WIE HEISST DER JUNGE? WIE HEISST DAS MÄDCHEN?

Because you still do not know many of the boys and girls in your class, you ask someone to tell you their names.

Wie heisst der Junge?

Er heisst Stefan.

Und das Mädchen? Wie heisst sie?

Sie heisst Sabine.

B4 Übung • Wie heisst er? Wie heisst sie? 📼

1. Ulrike

2. Lars

3. Natalie

4. Andreas

B5 WIE SAGT MAN DAS?
Asking and giving names

QUESTION	ANSWER
Wie heisst du? What's your name?	Ich heisse Andreas. My name is Andreas.
Wie heisst der Junge? What's the boy's name?	Er heisst Stefan. His name is Stefan.
Wie heisst das Mädchen? What's the girl's name?	Sie heisst Sabine. Her name is Sabine.

B6 Übung • Partnerarbeit *Teamwork*

Team up with a classmate. Ask each other the names of several other students in your class.

B7 Schreibübung • Wie heissen deine Mitschüler?

You are new in the class and want to find out the names of your new classmates. Rewrite each dialog, filling in the missing words.

A: Wie _____ du?
B: _____ _____ Andreas.

A: _____ heisst der Junge?
B: Er _____ Stefan.

A: Und das Mädchen? Wie _____ sie?
B: Sie _____ Ulrike.

A: Wie heisst _____ ?
B: Ich _____ _____ .

Here is another way of finding out who someone is.

> Wer ist das?

> Das ist der Stefan.

> Wer ist das?

> Das ist die Sabine.

> Und wer ist das?

> Das ist Herr Sperling, der Lehrer.

> Und das ist Frau Meier, die Lehrerin.

Herr Sperling, der Deutschlehrer

Frau Meier, die Deutschlehrerin

B9 WIE SAGT MAN DAS?
Asking who someone is

	QUESTION	ANSWER
		Das ist der Stefan. Das ist die Sabine. That's Stefan. That's Sabine.
	Wer ist das? Who is that?	Das ist Herr Sperling, der Deutschlehrer. That's Mr. Sperling, the German teacher.
		Das ist Frau Meier, die Deutschlehrerin. That's Mrs. Meier, the German teacher.

In everyday speech, the articles **der** and **die** are often used together with proper names when referring to other people, especially if you know the people well.

Ask a classmate to identify various people in your class, including your teacher.

    A: Wer ist das?
    B: Das ist . . .

B 11 ERKLÄRUNG *Explanation*
The Definite Articles **der, die, das**

German has three words for *the:* **der, die,** and **das,** called the definite articles. These words tell us which class (or gender) a German noun belongs to. For example, **der Junge,** *the boy,* belongs to a class called "masculine"; **die Lehrerin,** *the female teacher,* to a class called "feminine"; and **das Mädchen,** *the girl,* to a class called "neuter." You will learn more about this in Unit 2.

Masculine Nouns	Feminine Nouns	Neuter Nouns
der Junge **der Lehrer** **der Deutschlehrer**	**die Lehrerin** **die Deutschlehrerin**	**das Mädchen**

B 12 Schreibübung *Writing practice*

Rewrite the sentences, filling in the missing words.

1. Wie heisst _____ Junge?
2. _____ Lehrerin heisst Meier.
3. Das ist _____ Lehrer.
4. _____ Mädchen heisst Sabine.
5. Wie heisst _____ Deutschlehrerin?
6. Und _____ Deutschlehrer?

B 13 Übung · Ein Spiel *A game*

Do you know everyone in your class? Divide the class into two teams. The first student on Team A identifies himself or herself, saying **Ich heisse . . .** and then points to a student on the same team, asking **Wer ist das?** The first student on Team B must give the correct name. If the answer is correct, the student stays in the game. If it is incorrect, the student is out. Continue in this way, alternating teams.

B 14 Übung · Hör gut zu! *Listen carefully*

Are you referring to a girl or a boy? To a woman or a man?

	0	1	2	3	4	5	6	7	8
refers to a girl or a woman									
refers to a boy or a man	✔								

Übung · Ratespiel: Wer ist das? *Guessing game*

Bring in pictures of well-known people and ask the class to identify them.

A: Wer ist das? *or* A: Wie heisst er? Wie heisst sie?
B: Das ist . . .   B: Er heisst . . .   Sie heisst . . .

B 16 Ein wenig Landeskunde *A little culture*

In German, as in English, many family names reflect the occupation or characteristics of ancestors. Many family names were given to help identify people at a time when only first names were customary.

Wie heisst er? Er heisst

1. Fritz. . .

2. Herman. . .

3. Hans. . .

4. Gerhard. . .

5. Paul. . .

Müller
Gärtner
Schuhmacher
Bäcker
Fischer

Do you know someone with a German name? The United States' census of 1980 revealed that 27.4 percent of the population of the United States can claim German ancestry. It is therefore not surprising to find German family names in all parts of the United States, and there may be a number of students with a German name in your class. What German names do you know? In Germany today, the most common last name is **Müller.**

How old are your friends? How old are you?

C1 Wie alt bist du? 📼

Wie alt bist du?

Ich bin dreizehn Jahre alt.

Wie alt ist die Sabine?

Die Sabine ist fünfzehn.

Und wie alt ist der Stefan?

Der Stefan ist auch fünfzehn.

Wie alt sind Ulrike und Jochen?

Sie sind auch fünfzehn Jahre alt.

Jochen

Ulrike

Und wie alt bist du?
Ich bin _____ .

C2 Übung • Wie alt sind die Jungen und Mädchen?

1. Wie alt ist der Stefan?
2. Wie alt ist die Sabine?
3. Wie alt ist der Jochen?
4. Und die Ulrike?
5. Wie alt sind Stefan und Jochen?
6. Und wie alt bist du?

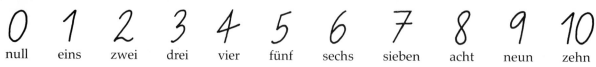
0 null *1* eins *2* zwei *3* drei *4* vier *5* fünf *6* sechs *7* sieben *8* acht *9* neun *10* zehn

11 elf *12* zwölf *13* dreizehn *14* vierzehn *15* fünfzehn *16* sechzehn *17* siebzehn *18* achtzehn *19* neunzehn *20* zwanzig

C4 Ein wenig Landeskunde

Notice in C3 how the numerals are written in German. Pay particular attention to the numerals *1* and *7*.

When using hand signals to indicate numbers, you use the thumb to indicate one, the thumb and the index finger to indicate two, and so on.

C5 Übung • Wir üben mit Zahlen

1. Count off in sequence: first student, **eins,** second student, **zwei,** etc.
2. Choose one student to count aloud all the boys and all the girls.
3. Complete each sequence of numbers. Say the numbers aloud in German.

   3, 4, 5, _____   drei, vier, fünf, sechs

   1. 9, 10, 11, _____
   2. 16, 17, 18, _____
   3. 1, 2, 3, _____
   4. 11, 12, 13, _____
   5. 2, 4, 6, _____
   6. 12, 14, 16, _____
   7. 6, 8, 10, _____
   8. 14, 16, 18, _____
   9. 5, 4, 3, _____
   10. 10, 9, 8, _____
   11. 20, 19, 18, _____
   12. 6, 5, 4, _____

4. Tell the class your phone number in German. Your classmates should write it down as you say it.

   Meine Telefonnummer ist . . .

C6 Übung • Zahlenlotto *Number Lotto*

Draw a rectangle and divide it into twenty squares as shown. Number the squares from 1 to 20 in any order you choose. Use each number only once. One student calls numbers from 1 to 20 in random order. As you hear each number, mark the corresponding square. The winner is the first one to fill in a horizontal line.

8	2	5	13	14
7	1	6	4	15
9	10	3	19	17
18	11	16	12	20

Asking someone's age and telling yours

	QUESTION	ANSWER
	Wie alt bist du? *How old are you?*	Ich bin dreizehn Jahre alt. *I'm thirteen years old.*
	Wie alt ist der Stefan? *How old is Stefan?*	Er ist fünfzehn. *He is fifteen.*
	Wie alt ist die Sabine? *How old is Sabine?*	Sie ist fünfzehn Jahre alt. *She's fifteen years old.*
	Wie alt sind Ulrike und Jochen? *How old are Ulrike and Jochen?*	Sie sind auch fünfzehn. *They are also fifteen.*

C8 ERKLÄRUNG *Explanation*

Personal Pronouns and the Verb sein

The phrases **ich bin, du bist, er ist, sie ist,** and **sie sind** each contain a subject pronoun corresponding to the English *I, you, he, she,* and *they,* plus a form of the verb **sein,** *to be: I am, you are, he/she/it is, they are.* **Sein** is one of the most frequently used verbs in German. The chart shows the plural forms **wir,** *we,* and **ihr,** *you* (plural), but you do not need to use them yet.

Singular			*Plural*		
Ich	**bin**		Wir	**sind**	
Du	**bist**		Ihr	**seid**	
Der Stefan Er	**ist**	15 Jahre alt.	Stefan and Sabine Sie	**sind**	15 Jahre alt.
Die Sabine Sie	**ist**				

C9 Übung • Wie alt sind die Schüler? —Vierzehn.

Everyone in this group is 14 years old.

> A: Wie alt ist der Fritz?
> B: Er ist vierzehn.

1. Wie alt ist der Hans?
2. Wie alt ist die Monika?
3. Wie alt sind Hans und Monika?

4. Wie alt ist der Günter?
5. Wie alt ist die Ulrike?
6. Wie alt sind Günter and Ulrike?

C10 Übung • Und wie alt sind diese Schüler?

The young people in each pair are the same age.

> A: Der Jochen ist fünfzehn. Und die Ulrike?
> B: Sie ist auch fünfzehn.

1. Die Sabine ist 15. Und der Stefan?
2. Der Andreas ist 11. Und die Erika?
3. Dieter and Petra sind 16. Und Peter und Monika?

4. Die Katrin ist 15. Und der Kurt?
5. Der Michael ist 17. Und die Helga?
6. Die Karin und der Bernd sind 13. Und der Hans und die Sabine?

C11 Übung • Hör gut zu!

Which sentences refer to a girl and which to a boy? Listen.

	0	1	2	3	4	5	6	7	8
Junge	✔								
Mädchen									

C12 Übung • Jetzt bist du dran

Your teacher has asked you to introduce three students to the class, giving their names and ages. First ask each of the three students, and then introduce them to the class.

> A: Wie heisst du? Wie alt bist du?
> B: Ich heisse . . . Ich bin . . .
> A: Das ist . . . Er ist . . . Sie ist . . .

C13 Schreibübung

1. Which verb form is missing?
  1. Wer _____ das?
  2. Das _____ Sabine.
  3. Sie _____ 14 Jahre alt.
  4. Wie alt _____ du?
  5. Peter und Ulrike _____ vierzehn.
  6. Ich _____ . . .

2. Write the numbers.
  1. Write your phone number, using German numerals.
  2. In German, dictate your phone number to a classmate. Have him or her write it down and read it back to you. Reverse roles.
  3. Now do the same thing with your ZIP code.

Now you will meet some young people from the German-speaking countries.

D1

Woher bist du?

Ich heisse Jens Kröger. Ich bin sechzehn Jahre alt. Ich bin aus Niebüll, aus Deutschland.

Ich bin die Wiebke Nedel. Ich bin fünfzehn. Ich bin auch aus Deutschland, aus Neuss.

Jens Kröger, 16
Niebüll, Deutschland

Wiebke Nedel, 15
Neuss, Deutschland

Ich heisse Dastl, Margit Dastl. Ich bin vierzehn. Ich bin aus Wien, aus Österreich.

Ich heisse Bruno Schmidlin. Ich bin auch fünfzehn. Ich bin aus der Schweiz, aus Zimmerwald.

Margit Dastl, 14
Wien, Österreich

Bruno Schmidlin, 15
Zimmerwald, Schweiz

Ich bin Kurt Langer. Ich bin 15.
Ich bin aus der DDR, aus Dresden.

Und woher bist du? Aus Kansas City? Aus Harrisburg? Aus Dallas? Ich bin aus _____.

Kurt Langer, 15
Dresden, DDR

Neue Freunde 45

Take a look at the map, and locate where our friends live. Say where each one is from.

SCHWEDEN

DÄNEMARK

NORDSEE

OSTSEE

Niebüll

Jens Kröger

POLEN

NIEDERLANDE

Neuss

DEUTSCHE
DEMOKRATISCHE
REPUBLIK

BELGIEN

Wiebke Nedel

Dresden

Kurt Langer

LUXEMBURG

BUNDESREPUBLIK
DEUTSCHLAND

TSCHECHOSLOWAK

FRANKREICH

Wien

Zimmerwald

SCHWEIZ

ÖSTERREICH

Bruno Schmidlin

LIECHTENSTEIN

Margit Dastl

ITALIEN

Übung • Schau auf die Karte! Woher ist . . .?

Look at the map and pictures on the preceding page and ask a classmate where the different young people are from.

A: Woher ist Jens?
B: Er ist aus Niebüll.

A: Wer ist aus Wien?
B: Margit Dastl ist aus Wien.

D4   WIE SAGT MAN DAS?
      Talking about where you are from

QUESTION	ANSWER
Jens, woher bist du?	Ich bin aus Deutschland. Aus Niebüll.
Jens, where are you from?	I'm from Germany. From Niebüll.
Woher ist Wiebke?	Sie ist aus Deutschland.
Woher ist Margit?	Margit ist aus Österreich.
Woher ist Bruno?	Er ist aus der Schweiz.
Woher ist Kurt?	Er ist aus der DDR.

D5   Übung • Jetzt bist du dran

1. Say hello to a classmate you haven't met yet. Ask his or her name and age and where he or she is from.
2. Introduce your new friend to the class. Give his or her name and age, and tell where he or she is from.
3. Talk about the girl or boy in each picture, telling the name and age and where she or he is from.

1.   2.   3.   4.   5.

4. Now introduce yourself, giving your name and age and where you are from.

D6   Schreibübung • Etwas über deine Freunde, etwas über dich

1. Pick two of the new friends you met in D1 and write a few sentences about each one, telling the name and age and where he or she is from.
2. Write a few sentences about yourself.

   Ich heisse . . .

Let's listen to how our friends answer the following questions.

Jörg fragt Jens:

Heisst du Michael?

Bist du aus Niebüll?

Nein, ich heisse Jens.

Ja.

Jörg fragt Lars:

Ist das der Jens?
Heisst er Nedel?
Ist er aus Niebüll?

Ja.
Nein, er heisst Kröger.
Ja, er ist aus Niebüll.

D8 ERKLÄRUNG
Asking and Answering Questions

1. There are questions that begin with a question word like **wer?,** *who?,* **wie?,** *how?,* and **woher?,** *from where?*

Questions beginning with a question word	Answers
Wer ist das?	Das ist Jens.
Wie alt ist er?	Er ist sechzehn.
Woher ist er?	Er ist aus Deutschland.

2. There are also questions that begin with verbs. Such questions anticipate answers that start with **ja,** *yes,* or **nein,** *no.*

Questions beginning with a verb	Answer
Heisst du Michael?	Nein.
	Nein, ich heisse Jens.
Bist du aus Niebüll?	Ja.
	Ja, ich bin aus Niebüll.
Ist er 16 Jahre alt?	Ja, er ist 16.

D 9   Übung · Jetzt bist du dran

Ask different classmates questions about themselves, anticipating *yes* or *no* answers.

Heisst du . . .?   Bist du fünfzehn?   Bist du aus . . .?

D 10   Übung · Wer ist dein Partner?

Write an age from 13 to 15 and the name of one of the cities in a German-speaking country on an index card and put the card in your pocket. Mingle with your classmates and try to find a partner whose card has information that matches your own. Be sure to ask and answer in German.

D 11   Übung · Hör gut zu!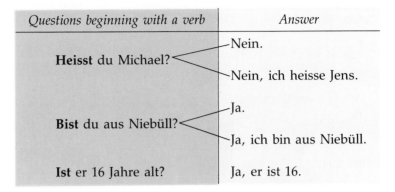

Questions and answers. Which ones go together? Listen.

	Ex.	Sie ist aus Deutschland.	3	Sie ist fünfzehn.
1		Ich bin vierzehn.	4	Das ist Jens Kröger.
2		Er heisst Michael.	5	Ich bin aus der Schweiz.

D 12   Schreibübung · Was sagt er? Was sagt sie?

Rewrite each dialog, supplying appropriate lines.

SCHÜLER 1	Guten Morgen!
SCHÜLER 2	_____
SCHÜLER 1	Wer ist das?
SCHÜLER 2	_____
SCHÜLER 1	Woher ist er/sie?
SCHÜLER 2	_____

FRAU MEIER	_____
SCHÜLER	Guten Tag, Frau Meier!
FRAU MEIER	_____
SCHÜLER	Das ist die Wiebke Nedel.
FRAU MEIER	_____
SCHÜLER	Sie ist aus Neuss.

Sometimes you do not quite hear or understand what someone has said and need the information repeated. How do you do this?

D 14   WIE SAGT MAN DAS?
What to say if you don't understand

If you have not heard or understood what someone has said, you ask for the information to be repeated. In German, this is generally done with **Wie bitte?** or more specifically, with a word such as **wer?,** *who?* or **woher?,** *from where?,* or by repeating the key word. Make sure to raise the tone of your voice.

You did not understand what was said and ask for the entire statement to be repeated.	Der Stefan ist aus Oberpfaffenhofen.	Wie bitte?	I beg your pardon?
You did not understand part of what was said and ask only for a part to be repeated.	Er ist aus Wien. Das ist der Lehrer. Wie alt ist der Stefan? Wie heisst du?	Woher? Wer ist das? Der Stefan? Ich?	From where? Who is that? Stefan? Me?

Übung · Jetzt bist du dran

A classmate makes a statement or asks a question, and you ask that person to repeat the information that you did not understand. Your classmate then gives an appropriate response.

> A: Sabine ist 15 Jahre alt.
> B: Wer? *or* Wie alt? *or* Wie bitte?
> A: Sabine. *or* Fünfzehn. *or* Sabine ist 15 Jahre alt.

D 16 WIE HEISSEN SIE? WOHER SIND SIE?

How do you ask your teacher some of the questions you have been asking your classmates? When you talk to your teacher and to most other adults outside your family, you use the **Sie**-form.

D 17 Übung · Frag deinen Lehrer! *Ask your teacher!*

1. Wie heissen Sie?
2. Woher sind Sie? Sind Sie aus Deutschland?

D 18 Übung · Guten Tag! Ich heisse . . .

Pick a German first and last name for yourself. Then select a city in one of the German-speaking countries as your home town. Tell the class who you are now.

Now you know how to greet people, to talk a little about yourself, and to ask others about themselves. Here are some more opportunities to use what you have learned.

1 Zwei Briefe 📼

It is fun to have a pen pal. As you continue your study of German, perhaps you, too, will have a pen pal. Imagine that these letters are for you.

Lieber Eric!

Ich heisse Petra Schmitt.
Ich bin aus Salzburg. Das
ist in Österreich. Ich bin
15 Jahre alt.
    Woher bist Du? Wie alt
bist Du? Bitte schreib mir!

            Viele Grüsse
            Petra

Liebe Mary!

Ich heisse Günter Weiss.
Ich bin aus Frankfurt.
Frankfurt ist in Deutschland.
Ich bin 14 Jahre alt.
    Woher bist Du? Wie alt
bist Du?

            Viele Grüsse
            Günter

Look at these letters. How do they start? Why do you think the greetings are spelled differently? How is the word **Du** spelled?

2 Übung • Woher ist das Mädchen? Wer ist der Junge?

1. Wie heisst das Mädchen?
2. Woher ist sie?
3. Wie alt ist sie?
4. Wie heisst der Junge?
5. Woher ist er?
6. Wie alt ist er?

3   Übung · Brieffreunde   *Pen Pals*

You choose a pen pal and a pen pal chooses you!

1. Write a letter like one of the sample letters, introducing yourself in German to a pen pal in a German-speaking country.
2. Write a letter that one of our friends from abroad (p. 45) might have written to you.

4   Übung · Du triffst neue Freunde. Was sagst du?
        You meet new friends. What do you say?

Imagine that you are staying at a youth hostel in Germany. A youth hostel is an inexpensive hotel for young people. While there, you meet several of our young German-speaking friends pictured on page 45. Exchange greetings and tell one another something about yourselves—for example, your name and age and where you are from.

5   Schreibübung · Unsere Freunde

Write a brief paragraph about the five friends from abroad. Write their names and ages and where they are from.

6   Aussprache-, Lese- und Schreibübungen
        Pronunciation, Reading, and Writing Exercises

1. Listen carefully and repeat what you hear.

2. Listen, then read aloud.
   ich, acht, dich, auch; alt, elf, null; wie, wer, Wien, wir,
   wo, woher, Wiedersehen; Zahl, zwei, zehn, Schweiz

3. Copy the following sentences to prepare yourself to write them from dictation.
   1. Wo ist Wien?
   2. Wie alt ist Michael?
   3. Zehn und zwei ist zwölf.
   4. Ich bin auch elf.

WAS KANNST DU SCHON?

Let's review some important points that you have learned in this unit.

SECTION A

Can you greet young people and adults in German?
Say hello to the following people:

1. Katrin	**3.** Mr. Sperling	**5.** Mrs. Meier
2. Stefan	**4.** Miss Seifert	**6.** your teacher

Can you say goodbye in German?
Say goodbye to the same people.

SECTION B

Can you introduce yourself in German?

1. Say hello.
2. Give your name.
3. Ask a classmate his or her name.

Can you find out who someone is?

1. Ask a boy's name, then tell it to someone else.
2. Ask a girl's name, then tell it to someone else.
3. Ask who someone is and give the answer.

SECTION C

Can you ask someone's age and tell yours?
Write a question and answer about age for each of the following pronouns:
    ich, du, er, sie, sie (plural).

Do you know the numbers from 0 to 20?
Write out in German the numbers from 0 to 20.

Do you know the forms of the verb *sein*?
Complete the following sentences.

1. Das Mädchen _____ 15.	**5.** _____ du aus Deutschland?
2. Ich _____ 13.	**6.** Wer _____ das?
3. Der Junge _____ 16.	**7.** Jens und Wiebke _____ aus Deutschland.
4. Frl. Seifert _____ aus Wien.	**8.** Er _____ aus Österreich.

SECTION D

Can you say where you are from? Can you ask where others are from?
Say where you are from. Ask one of your classmates where he or she is from.

Can you ask questions anticipating a yes or no answer?
Make up three questions anticipating a yes or no answer.

Can you ask for information to be repeated?
What do you say if you don't understand part or all of the following statements?

1. Ich bin aus Deutschland.	**3.** Das Mädchen ist 15 Jahre alt.
2. Er heisst Jens Kröger.	**4.** Der Deutschlehrer heisst Sperling.

Can you address adults using the *Sie*-form?
Ask your teacher his or her name and where he or she is from.

WORTSCHATZ *Vocabulary*

SECTION A

auf Wiedersehen! *goodbye!*
bis dann! *see you later!*
Frau *Mrs.*
Fräulein *Miss*
Frl. = Fräulein *Miss*
grüss dich! *hi!*
guten Morgen! *good morning!*
guten Tag! *hello!*
hallo! *hello! hi!*
Herr *Mr.*
Morgen! *morning!*
Tag! *hello! hi!*
tschau! *bye! so long!*
tschüs! *bye, so long!*
Wiedersehen! *bye!*

SECTION B

das *the; that*
das ist . . . *that's . . .*
der *the*
der **Deutschlehrer** *the German teacher* (m)
die **Deutschlehrerin** *the German teacher* (f)
die *the*
er heisst *his name is*
ich heisse *my name is*
der **Junge** *the boy*
der **Lehrer** *the teacher* (m)
die **Lehrerin** *the teacher* (f)
das **Mädchen** *the girl*
sie heisst *her name is*

und *and*
wer? *who?*
wer ist das? *who's that?*
wie heisst das Mädchen? *what's the girl's name?*
wie heisst der Junge? *what's the boy's name?*
wie heisst du? *what's your name?*
wie heisst er? *what's his name?*
wie heisst sie? *what's her name?*

SECTION C

alt *old*
auch *also*
du bist *you are*
er ist *he is*
ich bin *I am*
ich bin dreizehn. *I am thirteen.*
ich bin sechzehn Jahre alt. *I am sixteen years old.*
sie ist *she is*
sie sind *they are*
wie? *how?*
wie alt bist du? *how old are you?*
die **Zahlen** *the numbers*
die **Zahlen von null bis zwanzig** *the numbers from zero to twenty, see page 42*

SECTION D

aus *from*
aus der Schweiz *from Switzerland*
DDR = Deutsche Demokratische Republik *German Democratic Republic*[1]
Deutschland *Germany*
fragt *asks*
heissen Sie Müller? *is your name Müller?*
heisst du Michael? *is your name Michael?*
ich? *me?*
ich bin aus *I'm from*
ja *yes*
der **Mathematiklehrer** *the math teacher*
München *Munich*
nein *no*
oder *or*
Österreich *Austria*
Schweiz *Switzerland*
wie bitte? *I beg your pardon?*
wie heissen Sie? *what's your name?*
Wien *Vienna*
woher? *from where?*
woher bist du? *where are you from?*
woher sind . . .? *where are . . . from?*
woher sind Sie? *where are you from?*

---

[1]German words are usually stressed on the first syllable. When this is not the case, it will be indicated on the vocabulary list so you will know how to pronounce the word. The stress will be marked by an underscore or a dot. In addition to stress, the underscore will signify a long vowel; the dot will signify a short vowel.

WORTSCHATZÜBUNGEN *Vocabulary Activities*

1. All German nouns begin with a capital letter. Look at the **Wortschatz** and pick out all the nouns.

2. German has several letters that do not exist in English: **ä, ö, ü,** and **äu.** The marking ¨ is called an umlaut. Look at the **Wortschatz** above. Pick out all the words that have an umlaut, write them down, and say them.

Wo ist Deutschland?

Deutschland ist in Europa. Deutschland: das sind zwei Länder°, die Bundesrepublik Deutschland (BRD) und die Deutsche Demokratische Republik (DDR).

Die Bundesrepublik Deutschland hat° neun Nachbarn°: die Deutsche Demokratische Republik, die Tschechoslowakei, Österreich, die Schweiz, Frankreich, Luxemburg, Belgien, die Niederlande und Dänemark.

Wo ist Dänemark?—Dänemark ist nördlich von° Deutschland. Die Deutsche Demokratische Republik und die Tschechoslowakei sind östlich°, Österreich und die Schweiz sind südlich°, und Frankreich, Luxemburg, Belgien und die Niederlande sind westlich von° Deutschland.

Margit Dastl ist aus Wien. Wien ist die Hauptstadt° von Österreich. Die Hauptstadt der Bundesrepublik Deutschland ist Bonn. Berlin (Ost) ist die Hauptstadt der Deutschen Demokratischen Republik, und Bern ist die Hauptstadt der Schweiz.

Man spricht Deutsch° in Deutschland: in der Bundesrepublik und in der Deutschen Demokratischen Republik. Man spricht Deutsch auch in Österreich, in der Schweiz, in Liechtenstein (zwischen° Österreich und der Schweiz), auch in einem Teil von° Luxemburg und in Norditalien (in Südtirol).

Think about what you have read. What information could you give to someone who asked you "Where is Germany?" What else could you tell him or her?

Übung • Beantworte die Fragen! *Answer the questions.*

1. Wo ist Deutschland?
2. Wie heissen die Nachbarn?
3. Wo ist Österreich? Und Frankreich?
4. Welche° Nachbarn sind westlich der Bundesrepublik? Und östlich? Südlich?
5. Was ist Wien? Berlin (Ost)? Bern? Bonn?
6. Wo spricht man Deutsch?
7. Wo spricht man Deutsch in den Vereinigten Staaten°?
8. Wie heissen unsere Nachbarn?
9. Und wie heisst unsere Hauptstadt?

---

wo *where;* **Länder** *countries;* **hat** *has;* **Nachbarn** *neighbors;* **nördlich von** *north of;* **östlich** *east (of);* **südlich** *south (of);* **westlich von** *west of;* **die Hauptstadt** *the capital;* **man spricht Deutsch** *German is spoken;* **zwischen** *between;* **in einem Teil von** *in a part of;* **welche** *which;* **in den Vereinigten Staaten** *in the United States*

Read the following statements. If a statement is true, say **Stimmt!** If a statement is false, say **Stimmt nicht!** Then correct it.

1. England ist mitten in Europa.
2. Wien ist die Hauptstadt Österreichs.
3. Dänemark liegt nördlich von Deutschland.
4. Die Hauptstadt der DDR ist Bern.
5. Die Schweiz liegt östlich von Österreich.
6. In der DDR spricht man Deutsch.
7. Österreich ist Frankreichs Nachbar.
8. Liechtenstein ist zwischen Österreich und der Schweiz.

Übung • Klassenprojekt *Class project*

Divide into groups of four to six students. Choose a country where German is the official language and do one or more of the following projects:

1. Draw a map of that country. Show the capital, the principal cities, the major rivers and mountains, and the boundaries.
2. Draw and color the flag of that country.
3. Try to find some magazine and newspaper articles and photos pertaining to that country. Make a cultural scrapbook or a bulletin board.
4. Collect recipes from that country and compile a cookbook. If possible, prepare some of the recipes for the class.

Postkarten

Our new friends are traveling. Here are some postcards they sent to their friends.

Schweiz . Suisse . Svizzera
Bern - Hauptstadt der Schweiz

Herzliche Grüsse aus der Schweiz. Ich bin in Bern.
Wiebke

Frl. Katja Hauser
Haupts... 17
7840

Wien . Vienna
Parlament

Grüss dich!
Ich bin in Österreich, in Wien!
Tschüs, Bruno

Herrn Michael Pertsch
Bahnhofstrasse 38
4790 Paderborn

Übung • Jetzt bist du dran!

Now write in German a postcard to a friend back home from one or all of the following places: Wien, Dresden, Hamburg, Innsbruck.

KAPITEL 2
Schule

In this unit you will meet some high school students from German-speaking countries. About 35 percent of the young people between the ages of 10 and 19 attend academic high schools, and many, though not all, will continue to a university or to another school of higher learning.

In this unit you will:

SECTION A	tell how you get to school
SECTION B	talk about school supplies and how much they cost
SECTION C	talk about your class schedule, tell time
SECTION D	talk about homework and grades
TRY YOUR SKILLS	use what you've learned
ZUM LESEN	read for practice and pleasure

These are the ways some of our friends from abroad get to school. Let's see if they are different from the way you get to school.

A1 Wie kommst du in die Schule?

A: Schau, da kommt der Jens mit dem Moped!
B: Toll!
A: Wie kommst du in die Schule?
B: Ich? Ich komme mit dem Bus. Und du?
A: Zu Fuss.

Der Jens kommt mit dem Moped.

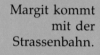

Margit kommt mit der Strassenbahn.

Die Wiebke kommt mit dem Rad.

Frl. Seifert kommt mit dem Auto.

Wer kommt zu Fuss?

A2 Übung • Beantworte die Fragen! *Answer the questions.*

1. Wie kommt Jens in die Schule?
2. Wie kommt Margit in die Schule?
3. Und Wiebke?

4. Wie kommt Frl. Seifert in die Schule?
5. Wer kommt mit dem Moped?

WIE SAGT MAN DAS?
Saying how you get to school

The verb **kommen** can have different meanings.

Schau, da kommt der Jens mit dem Moped.	Look, here comes Jens on his moped.
Wie kommt Margit in die Schule?	How does Margit get to school?
Margit kommt mit der Strassenbahn.	Margit comes by streetcar.
Wer kommt zu Fuss?	Who walks?

A4 Übung • Und du? Wie steht's mit dir? *And what about you?*

1. Wie kommst du in die Schule?
2. Wer kommt mit dem Rad?
3. Wer kommt mit dem Bus?
4. Wer kommt zu Fuss?

A5 ERKLÄRUNG
The Verb kommen

The verb **kommen** has the following forms. You do not have to use **wir,** *we,* and **ihr,** *you* (plural) yet.

Singular			Plural		
Ich	**komme**		Wir	**kommen**	
Du	**kommst**	mit dem Rad.	Ihr	**kommt**	mit dem Rad.
Jens (er) Karin (sie)	**kommt** **kommt**		Jens und Karin (sie)	**kommen**	

A6 Übung • Jetzt bist du dran

1. You are conducting a survey for your teacher. Go around the class and find out how everyone gets to school.

   A: Wie kommst du in die Schule?
   B: Ich komme . . .

2. Now tell your teacher how everybody gets to school.

   Der Peter kommt . . .   Die Barbara kommt . . .
   Der Paul, der Martin, die Mary und die Heidi kommen . . .

A7 Übung • Wie kommen alle in die Schule?

Mit dem Bus:	*10*
Mit . . .	

1. Pick four classmates and one of your teachers and write sentences telling how each one gets to school.
2. Make a chart showing how your classmates get to school. Report your findings to the class.

asking about prices of school supplies

At the beginning of the school year, everyone has to buy school supplies. Jens goes to a store where school supplies are displayed in the window. He goes inside and asks about prices. What supplies do you need for school?

Schulsachen

Wörterbuch
DM 13,00

Schultasche
DM 20,00

Bleistift   Kuli
DM 1,00   DM 4,00

Kassette
DM 6,00

Stundenplan
DM 1,10

Heft
DM 1,20

Taschenrechner
DM 18,00

Poster
DM 5,00

JENS	Entschuldigung! Was kostet das Wörterbuch, bitte?
VERKÄUFERIN	Das Wörterbuch? —Dreizehn Mark.
JENS	Und was kostet der Taschenrechner?
VERKÄUFERIN	Achtzehn Mark.
JENS	Wie bitte?
VERKÄUFERIN	Achtzehn Mark.
JENS	Prima, nur achtzehn Mark! Und was kostet die Kassette?
VERKÄUFERIN	Sechs Mark.
JENS	Danke!
VERKÄUFERIN	Bitte!

The German unit of currency is the **Deutsche Mark,** abbreviated **DM.** One **Mark** has one hundred **Pfennige.** Prices are usually indicated in the following way: **DM** in front of the price, and a comma separating **Mark** and **Pfennig.** In advertising material, a period is often used instead of a comma. Here is how to read prices:

DM 1,00	*reads*	eine Mark
DM 1,10		eine Mark zehn
DM 2,00		zwei Mark
DM 6,18		sechs Mark achtzehn

B3   Übung • Wir lesen Preise!

Read the following prices.

1. DM 11,00	**4.** DM 9,00	**7.** DM 1,17
2. DM 2,10	**5.** DM 7,05	**8.** DM 19,00
3. DM 17,20	**6.** DM 13,08	**9.** DM 4,02

B4   Übung • Was kostet alles?

What does each item pictured on page 64 cost?

    A: Was kostet das Heft?
    B: Das Heft? Eine Mark zwanzig.

1. Was kostet die Schultasche?
2. Was kostet der Stundenplan?
3. Und das Wörterbuch?
4. Was kostet der Taschenrechner?

5. Und die Kassette?
6. Was kostet der Kuli?
7. Und was kostet das Poster?
8. Und der Bleistift?

B5   Übung • Hör gut zu!

How much does it cost? Listen.

0	1	2	3	4	5	6	7	8	9	10
3,10										

B6   ERKLÄRUNG
The Definite Articles der, die, das

When Jens asked about the price of various school supplies, you noticed that he used different words with every noun. He said **das Wörterbuch, der Taschenrechner, die Kassette,** and so on. These words are called definite articles. They name something specific or definite.   *(continued)*

There are three genders of German nouns: masculine, feminine, and neuter. The definite articles **der, die,** and **das** tell you the gender—they are gender markers. The gender marker **der** tells you **der Bleistift,** *the pencil,* is masculine; **die** tells you **die Schultasche,** *the schoolbag,* is feminine; **das** tells you **das Heft,** *the notebook,* is neuter. Since usually there is no other way of telling the gender of a noun, you must remember each noun with its gender marker, the definite article.

Nouns for people are generally masculine for males **(der Junge)** and feminine for females **(die Lehrerin).** There are a few exceptions, such as **das Mädchen,** *the girl,* which is neuter because of its ending, **-chen.** All nouns with the ending **-chen** are neuter.

Here is a list of the nouns that you have learned so far. Study them with their gender markers.

Masculine	Feminine	Neuter
der Lehrer	die Frau	das Mädchen
der Junge	die Lehrerin	das Heft
der Kuli	die Verkäuferin	das Poster
der Bleistift	die Zahl	das Wörterbuch
der Stundenplan	die Schule	
der Taschenrechner	die Schultasche	
	die Kassette	

B7   Übung · Was kostet . . .?

Your friend wants to know what each item costs. Tell him or her.

1. Das Heft kostet DM 1,20.   **2.** Der Taschenrechner . . .

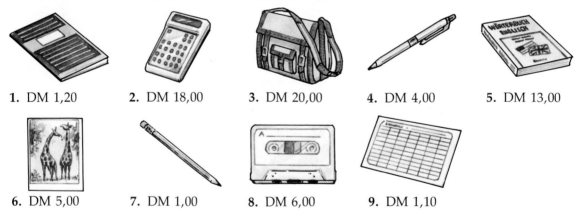

1. DM 1,20   **2.** DM 18,00   **3.** DM 20,00   **4.** DM 4,00   **5.** DM 13,00

6. DM 5,00   **7.** DM 1,00   **8.** DM 6,00   **9.** DM 1,10

B8   WIE SAGT MAN DAS?
Saying please, thank you, and you're welcome

The word **bitte** means both *please* and *you're welcome.*

Das Poster, bitte!	The poster, please.
Danke!	Thank you.
Bitte!	You're welcome.

B9 Übung • Rollenspiel *Role playing*

Lay out various school supplies (a pen, a notebook, and so on) on a table. Make a price tag for each item and turn it face down. Take turns with classmates playing salesperson and customer. Practice polite exchanges: the customer asks the price of an item, the salesperson looks it up and answers. Don't forget to say please, thank you, and you're welcome.

> A: Was kostet das Poster, bitte?
> B: Das Poster kostet sieben Mark.
> A: Danke!
> B: Bitte!

B10 Übung • Hör gut zu!

Is the noun masculine, feminine, or neuter? Listen.

	0	1	2	3	4	5	6	7	8	9	10
masculine											
feminine	✔										
neuter											

B11 Schreibübung • Im Laden *In the store*

You want to buy a dictionary, a schoolbag, and a pocket calculator. You are asking the salesperson for prices. Write out your conversation. Be polite!

B12 WAS KOSTEN DIE SCHULSACHEN?

Bücher
DM 8,00

Taschenrechner
DM 18,00

SCHREIBGERÄTE

Kassetten
DM 6,00

Kulis
DM 4,00

Poster
DM 5,00

Bleistifte
DM 1,00

B 13 Übung • Was kostet alles?

1. Was kosten die Kassetten?
2. Was kosten die Poster?
3. Und die Bücher?

4. Was kosten die Taschenrechner?
5. Was kosten die Bleistifte?
6. Und was kosten die Kulis?

B 14 ERKLÄRUNG
Noun Plurals

1. There is no gender distinction in the plural. The definite article used with all plural nouns is **die**.

Singular	Plural
der Kuli	Kulis
die Kassette →die–	Kassetten
das Poster	Poster

2. The plural form of most German nouns is not predictable from the singular form and must be learned for each noun. The following list shows you the plural forms of the German nouns that you have learned so far. Each noun is listed with its definite article and its plural form.

Singular	Plural		Singular	Plural	
der Bleistift	die Bleistifte	-e	das Buch	die Bücher	¨er
das Heft	die Hefte	-e	das Wörterbuch	die Wörterbücher	¨er
der Stundenplan	die Stundenpläne	¨e	der Kuli	die Kulis	-s
der Junge	die Jungen	-n	der Lehrer	die Lehrer	-
die Kassette	die Kassetten	-n	das Mädchen	die Mädchen	-
die Schule	die Schulen	-n	das Poster	die Poster	-
die Schultasche	die Schultaschen	-n	der Taschenrechner	die Taschenrechner	-
die Zahl	die Zahlen	-en			
die Lehrerin	die Lehrerinnen	-nen			
die Verkäuferin	die Verkäuferinnen	-nen			

B 15 Übung • Singular und Plural

Say the article and the plural form for each of the following nouns.

A: Heft
B: das Heft, die Hefte

1. Bleistift
2. Lehrerin
3. Poster
4. Wörterbuch
5. Kuli
6. Mädchen
7. Schultasche
8. Junge
9. Buch
10. Kassette
11. Taschenrechner
12. Zahl
13. Lehrer
14. Schule
15. Verkäuferin

ERKLÄRUNG
Was kostet—was kosten

| asking for one item | Was **kostet** die Kassette? | *How much is the cassette?* |
| asking for more than one item | Was **kosten** die Bleistifte? | *How much are the pencils?* |

B 17 Übung · Jetzt bist du dran

You are in the store and are asking about prices.

> das Poster   Was kostet das Poster?
> die Bleistifte   Was kosten die Bleistifte?

1. die Schultasche
2. der Taschenrechner
3. die Kassetten
4. das Buch

5. die Bleistifte
6. das Wörterbuch
7. der Kuli
8. das Heft

B 18 Übung · Hör gut zu!

Singular or plural? Listen.

	0	1	2	3	4	5	6	7	8	9	10
singular	✔										
plural											

B 19 Schreibübung

1. Write the plural form of each of the following nouns.

> der Junge   die Jungen

1. das Mädchen
2. das Poster
3. das Wörterbuch
4. der Kuli

5. die Verkäuferin
6. der Bleistift
7. der Stundenplan
8. der Taschenrechner

2. Write each of the following questions in the plural.

> Was kostet das Poster?   Was kosten die Poster?

1. Was kostet das Heft?
2. Was kostet die Schultasche?
3. Was kostet das Buch?
4. Was kostet die Kassette?

5. Was kostet der Bleistift?
6. Was kostet der Taschenrechner?
7. Was kostet das Wörterbuch?
8. Was kostet der Stundenplan?

3. Write a dialogue that takes place in a **Schreibwarengeschäft.**

Get the salesperson's attention and ask for the prices of the
following items: pens, pencils, posters, cassettes, notebooks,
calculators, schoolbags, and dictionaries.

Du, Jens, wo ist das Wörterbuch?

Es ist dort drüben. Schau, Kristin, dort!

Du, Kristin, der Taschenrechner ist weg.

Unsinn! Er ist da.

Jens, wo ist die Kassette?

Ist sie nicht da?—Schau mal, Kristin! Hier ist sie.

Entschuldigung, Frau Meier! Wo sind die Poster, bitte?

Ich weiss nicht. Sind sie nicht da?

Nein, sie sind weg.

Weg? Schau mal, sie sind da drüben!

B 21 Übung • Wo ist . . .? 🖭

You are looking for the following items. Ask your teacher.

SCHÜLER Wo ist die Schultasche?
LEHRER Schau, sie ist hier. *or* Sie ist da. *or* Sie ist dort drüben.

1. Wo ist das Wörterbuch?
2. Wo sind die Poster?
3. Wo ist der Kuli?

4. Wo ist die Kassette?
5. Wo ist der Jens?
6. Wo ist die Kristin?

ERKLÄRUNG
The Pronouns er, sie, es, *and* sie *(plural)*

You can refer to noun phrases such as **der Taschenrechner, die Kassette, das Wörterbuch, die Poster,** using the words **er, sie,** and **es.** These words are called pronouns. The pronoun **er** refers to a masculine noun; **sie** refers to a feminine noun or a plural noun, and **es** refers to a neuter noun. Notice that **er, sie,** and **es**—when referring to things in the singular—all mean *it.*

		Noun Phrase		Pronoun	
Singular	Masculine Feminine Neuter	Wo ist	**der Taschenrechner?** **die Kassette?** **das Wörterbuch?**	**Er** ist dort drüben. **Sie** ist dort drüben. **Es** ist dort drüben.	*It is . . .*
Plural	(no gender)	Wo sind **die Poster?**		**Sie** sind dort drüben.	*They are . . .*

B 23 Übung • So eine Unordnung!

What a mess! You and your friend can't find anything. Help each other out.

> A: Die Schultasche ist weg!
> B: Unsinn! Sie ist hier!

1. Der Stundenplan ist weg!
2. Die Bleistifte sind weg!
3. Das Wörterbuch ist weg!
4. Die Kassette ist weg!
5. Die Hefte sind weg!
6. Der Kuli ist weg!
7. Das Poster ist weg!
8. Der Taschenrechner ist weg!

B 24 Übung • Die Schule beginnt. Wo ist . . .?

When you get to school, you ask a friend where the following people are.

> A: Wo ist Herr Sperling?
> B: Ist er nicht da?

1. Wo ist der Jens?
2. Wo sind Jens und Kristin?
3. Wo ist Frl. Seifert?
4. Wo ist der Deutschlehrer?
5. Wo ist das Mädchen[1]?
6. Wo ist der Junge?

---

[1]The pronoun **sie** is used to refer to **das Mädchen.**

B 25 WIE SAGT MAN DAS?
Getting someone's attention

Here are some expressions you can use to get someone's attention.

Entschuldigung!	Excuse me.
Du, Jens, . . .	Hey, Jens, . . .
Schau!	Look!
Schau, Jens!	Look, Jens!
Schau mal!	Take a look!
Schau mal, Kristin!	Take a look, Kristin!

1.

Wörterbuch
Kassetten
Taschenrechner
Bleistifte
Kuli
Schultasche
Heft

Here is a list of school supplies that have been misplaced.
A classmate is asking you about each of these items. You tell
where they are, or you may say that you don't know. Vary your
answers, using the words and phrases given on the right.

A: Du, Paul, wo ist
   das Wörterbuch?
B: Schau mal!
   Es ist hier.
A: Prima!

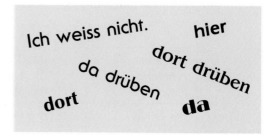

Ich weiss nicht.   hier
   dort drüben
da drüben
dort   da

2. You are looking at school supplies with a friend.
   Practice the following dialog,
   substituting the words given on the right.
   Give a price or say you don't know.

   A: Schau mal, Jens! Der Taschen-
      rechner ist prima!
   B: Du, was kostet er?
   A: . . .

Wörterbuch   Kassette
      Hefte   Kuli
Poster   Taschenrechner

3. You are asking for someone's name. Practice the
   following dialog, substituting a person listed
   on the right. Make up a name for each person.

   A: Entschuldigung! Wie heisst der
      Deutschlehrer?
   B: Er heisst Sperling.
   A: Ach ja, Sperling.

die Verkäuferin   der Junge

die Deutschlehrerin

der Lehrer   das Mädchen

Er, sie, or **es?** Listen.

	0	1	2	3	4	5	6	7	8	9	10	11	12
er													
sie	✔												
es													

Write a dialog that takes place in a store. The customer gets the salesperson's
attention and asks about the price of various school supplies. The salesperson
tells the prices, using pronouns to refer to the items. The customer thanks the
salesperson and he or she responds. Practice your dialog with a classmate.

German high school students in the upper grades must take a number of core subjects, and they are limited in their choice of minor subjects. Take a look at Jens' schedule, a typical ninth grade schedule, and compare it with your own.

C1 Welche Fächer hast du heute?

FRAU KRÖGER   Welche Fächer hast du heute?
JENS   Ich habe Mathe, Geschichte,
Moment mal! Schau, hier ist
der Stundenplan. Heute ist
Dienstag?
FRAU KRÖGER   Ja.
JENS   Ich habe um acht Uhr
Deutsch, um Viertel vor neun
Mathe.
Ich habe dann Englisch
und Geschichte.

Jens geht auf die Oberschule in Niebüll. Er hat von Montag bis Freitag Schule. Jens hat sonnabends frei. Die Schule beginnt um acht Uhr, und sie ist um ein Uhr aus.

Welche Fächer hat er? Hier ist Jens' Stundenplan.

Wann hast du Physik?

Am Freitag.

Zeit	Montag	Dienstag	Mittwoch	Donnerstag	Freitag	Samstag
8.00-8.40	Deutsch	Deutsch	Mathe	—	Physik	
8.45-9.30	Deutsch	Mathe	Deutsch	Physik	Mathe	
9.30-9.45	—		Pause			
9.45-10.30	Religion	Englisch	Englisch	Biologie	Deutsch	
10.30-11.15	Biologie	Englisch	Latein	Englisch	Latein	frei
11.15-11.30	—		Pause	—		
11.30-12.15	Latein	Geschichte	Sport	Geschichte	Kunst	
12.15-13.00	Musik	—	Sport	Geographie		

Stundenplan für *Jens Kröger* 9a

Ein wenig Landeskunde

Jens is in a high school that emphasizes science subjects: mathematics, physics, biology, and chemistry, a subject that Jens will start in the tenth grade. At the same time, Jens is required to take two foreign languages, English and Latin. As you can see, his class schedule varies from day to day, and he takes more subjects than you do. He does not have the same subject at the same time every day, nor does he always have the same subjects every day. Jens and his classmates stay together for all their classes, and for the most part, they stay in the same classroom, unless they go to the science lab, the art room, or the gym. In German schools, the teachers move from room to room. German students generally spend less time in school than American students. There are no study halls or lunch periods. After school there are few school-sponsored sports, clubs, or social activities.

C3 **Übung • Stimmt oder stimmt nicht?**

Check each of the following statements against Jens' class schedule. If a statement is true, say **Stimmt;** if it is not true, say **Stimmt nicht!**

1. Jens hat am Montag Latein.
2. Er hat am Dienstag Geographie.
3. Jens hat am Donnerstag Deutsch.
4. Er hat sonnabends frei.
5. Er hat am Dienstag um acht Uhr Deutsch, dann Latein und Sport.

C4 **Übung • Jens' Stundenplan**

1. Auf welche Schule geht Jens?
2. Wann hat Jens Schule?
3. Welche Fächer hat er am Montag?
4. Was hat er am Dienstag?
5. Welche Fächer hat er am Mittwoch?
6. Was hat er am Donnerstag?
7. Welche Fächer hat er am Freitag?
8. Was hat er sonnabends?
9. Wann beginnt die Schule?
10. Wann ist sie aus?

C5 **Übung • Und du? Wie steht's mit dir?**

1. Auf welche Schule gehst du?
2. Welche Fächer hast du?
3. Welche Fächer hast du am Montag?
4. Was hast du am Dienstag?
5. Wann hast du Deutsch?
6. Wann hast du frei?
7. Wann beginnt die Schule?
8. Wann ist sie aus?

C6 **ZAHLEN**

Let's count by fives.

5	*10*	*15*	*20*	*25*	*30*
fünf	zehn	fünfzehn	zwanzig	fünfundzwanzig	dreissig

35	*40*	*45*	*50*	*55*	*60*
fünfunddreissig	vierzig	fünfundvierzig	fünfzig	fünfundfünfzig	sechzig

 um ein Uhr
um eins

 um zwei Uhr
um zwei

Wie spät ist es? Es ist . . .

neun Uhr

neun Uhr fünf
fünf nach neun

neun Uhr zehn
zehn nach neun

neun Uhr fünfzehn
Viertel nach neun

neun Uhr zwanzig
zwanzig nach neun

neun Uhr fünfundzwanzig
fünfundzwanzig nach neun

neun Uhr dreissig
halb zehn

neun Uhr fünf-
unddreissig

neun Uhr vierzig

neun Uhr fünfundvierzig
Viertel vor zehn

neun Uhr fünfzig
zehn vor zehn

neun Uhr fünf-
undfünfzig
fünf vor zehn

See if you can express the following times in two different ways.

Es ist . . . oder . . .

1. 2. 3. 4. 5. 6.

Übung · Rollenspiel

Pretend you are Jens. Practice the following dialog with a classmate.

Montag um 10.30? MITSCHÜLER Was hast du am Montag um halb elf?
                       JENS Um halb elf? Moment mal! —Ich habe Biologie
                             um halb elf.

1. Dienstag um 8.45?   3. Mittwoch um 11.30?   5. Freitag um 9.45?
2. Um 11.15?   4. Montag um 11.45?   6. Montag um 8.00?

C10 WAS HABT IHR JETZT?

Jörg und Kristin sind Klassenkameraden. Sie gehen in die neunte Klasse, die 9a.

Mona und Lars sind auch Klassenkameraden. Sie gehen auch in die neunte Klasse, in die Parallelklasse, die 9b.

C11 Übung · Beantworte die Fragen!

1. Wer sind Lars und Mona?   3. Welches Fach haben sie jetzt?
2. In welche Klasse gehen sie?   4. Und Jörg und Kristin? Was haben sie jetzt?

C12 ERKLÄRUNG
The Verb haben

The verb **haben,** *to have,* has the following forms.

Ich	**habe**			Wir	**haben**	
Du	**hast**	Deutsch.		Ihr	**habt**	Deutsch.
Jens (er)	**hat**			Jens und Kristin (sie)	**haben**	
Kristin (sie)	**hat**					

Übung • Wer hat heute Deutsch?

Do all these students have German today? They do!

Jens?   Ja, er hat heute Deutsch.

1. Kristin?
2. Jörg und Kristin?
3. Du?
4. Der Junge?
5. Ihr?
6. Ich?
7. Das Mädchen?
8. Wir?

C14 Übung • Was haben die Schüler heute?

What courses do the students have? Use a different course in each answer.

Jörg?   Er hat Geschichte.

1. Ich?
2. Das Mädchen?
3. Der Junge?
4. Wir?
5. Lars und Mona?
6. Kristin?

C15 Übung • Hör gut zu!

What time is it?

							1		
6.50	12.30	9.35	1.10	10.40	11.45	4.15	7.20	2.25	8.45

C16 Übung • Partnerarbeit

Practice the following activities with a classmate.

1. Ask what time it is, and after he or she responds, say thank you. Begin by saying:
Wie spät ist es?

2. Tell what subjects you have and when you have them. Here are some additional subjects that you might have. Not all of them are taught in German high schools: Chemie, Sozialkunde (*social studies*), Naturwissenschaft (*science*), Algebra, Geometrie, Französisch, Spanisch, Zeichnen (*drawing*), Hauswirtschaftskunde (*home economics*), Werken (*industrial arts*), Musik, Schulorchester, Schulkapelle (*band*), Schulchor, Fahrunterricht (*driver's education*), Schreibmaschineschreiben (*typing*).

C17 Schreibübung

1. Rewrite each sentence, filling in the correct form of **haben.**

1. Ich _____ heute Deutsch.
2. Was _____ du heute?
3. Der Jens _____ jetzt Mathe.
4. Wir _____ jetzt auch Mathe.
5. Was _____ ihr dann?
6. Jens und Kristin _____ Biologie.

2. Write out what time it is.

5.10   Es ist fünf Uhr zehn (zehn nach fünf).

1. 2.30   2. 3.45   3. 7.10   4. 6.15   5. 9.30   6. 8.50

3. Write out your own class schedule, using German words for your subjects. How well do you know your schedule? Exchange schedules with a classmate and ask each other questions.
Wann hast du Geschichte? Was hast du am Dienstag um . . .?

talking about homework and grades

Homework takes up a large part of a student's afternoon. There is homework in many subjects, and students have to work hard to get good grades to stay in school.

D1 Hausaufgaben und Noten

Jens macht Hausaufgaben. Er macht Mathe. In Mathe ist Jens nicht so gut. Welche Noten hat er in Mathe? Eine Vier, eine Drei, eine Vier.

Was hast du?

Eine Eins!

Toll!

Prima!

Schade!

Blöd!

Zensuren-spiegel

Fächer	Noten			Halbj.-zeugn.	Noten			Jahres-zeugn.
Deutsch	2	2	1					
	2							
Englisch	1	1	2					
	1	1						
Mathe-matik	4	3	4					
~~Franz.~~ Latein	3	1	2					
	2							
Physik	3	2	2					
	1							
Chemie								
Biologie	1	2	2					
Erd-kunde	3	3						
Ge-schichte	4	1	2					
Musik	1	1						
Kunst	2	1						
Religion	1	2						

Hier sind Jens' Noten.

KRISTIN   Du, Jens, was hast du in Deutsch?
JENS   Eine Zwei.
KRISTIN   Das ist prima! Eine Zwei in Deutsch. Phantastisch!
JENS   Ja, das ist gut. Aber ich habe nur eine Vier in Mathe. Blöd!
KRISTIN   Ja, das ist schlecht. Schade!

In German schools, grades range from 1 to 6: 1 (sehr gut, *excellent*), 2 (gut, *good*), 3 (befriedigend, *satisfactory*), 4 (ausreichend, *just passing*), 5 (mangelhaft, *almost failing*), and 6 (ungenügend, *failing*)—corresponding to A, B, C, D, and F in American schools. On report cards, German students also receive grades in Betragen, *conduct*, Fleiss, *diligence*, Aufmerksamkeit, *attentiveness*, and Ordnung, *neatness*.

D3 Übung • Beantworte die Fragen!

1. Was macht Jens?
2. Ist er gut in Mathe?

3. Welche Noten hat er in Mathe?
4. Welche Noten hat er in Latein?

D4 Übung • Und du? Wie steht's mit dir?

1. Bist du gut in Mathe?
2. Was hast du in Mathe?

3. Welche Noten hast du in Deutsch?
4. Was hast du in Englisch?

D5 WIE SAGT MAN DAS?
Some ways of responding to good news and to bad news

good news	Gut!	Good!
	Prima!	Terrific!
	Phantastisch!	Fantastic!
	Toll!	Great!
bad news	Blöd!	Too dumb!
	Das ist nicht so gut.	That's not so good.
	Das ist schlecht.	That's bad!
	Schade!	Too bad!

D6 Übung • Jetzt bist du dran

Now ask your classmates what their grades are in different subjects and react to the good news or bad news. Then have a classmate ask you the same questions.

A: Was hast du in Biologie?
B: Ich habe eine. . .
A: . . . *or* . . .

D8   Übung · Jetzt bist du dran

A: Wie ist Bio? Schwer? Leicht?   B: Bio ist nicht schwer. Bio ist . . .

Geschichte   Bio   Physik

Deutsch   Latein   Geographie

Englisch   Mathe   Musik

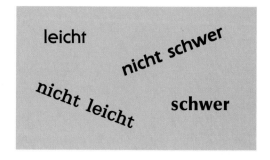

leicht

nicht schwer

nicht leicht   schwer

D9   Übung · Gut oder schlecht?

Choose a partner. React to each of the following statements made by your
partner. Use different expressions as you respond to good news or bad news.

A: Ich habe eine Zwei in Deutsch.
B: Das ist prima!

1. Ich habe eine Fünf in Physik.
2. Ich habe eine Drei in Mathe.
3. Ich habe eine Eins in Biologie.

4. Ich habe eine Vier in Geschichte.
5. Ich habe eine Sechs in Algebra.
6. Ich habe eine Zwei in Erdkunde.

Übung · Hör gut zu!

Is it good news or bad news? Listen.

	0	1	2	3	4	5	6	7	8	9	10
good news											
bad news	✔										

D 11 Schreibübung · Was meinst du? *What do you think?*

1. Write four short dialogs, asking friends about their grades and reacting to the good or bad news.

Peter, Geschichte, Vier

A: Was hat Peter in Geschichte?
B: Er hat eine Vier.
A: Das ist schade!

1. du, Deutsch, Eins
2. Barbara, Englisch, Fünf

3. Peter, Erdkunde, Sechs
4. Jens und Kristin, Latein, Zwei

2. Write sentences agreeing or disagreeing with each of the following statements.

A: Algebra ist schwer.
B: Ja, Algebra ist schwer.   *or*   Nein, Algebra ist nicht schwer.
        or   Nein, Algebra ist leicht.

1. Biologie ist leicht.
2. Kunst ist nicht leicht.
3. Deutsch ist toll.

4. Englisch ist schwer.
5. Geschichte ist nicht schwer.
6. Die Hausaufgaben sind schwer.

D 12 Übung · Wer hat gute Augen? *Who has good eyes?*

Was ist alles auf diesem Bild?   Und was fehlt hier?

1   Gerd Ecker in den USA

Gerd Ecker, a student from Germany, introduces himself to your class.

Guten Tag! Ich heisse Gerd Ecker. Ich bin 16 Jahre alt. Ich bin aus Paderborn. Paderborn ist in der Bundesrepublik Deutschland. Ich gehe aufs Goerdeler Gymnasium. Ich komme mit dem Rad in die Schule, und die Klassen- kameraden—ja, sie kommen mit dem Bus, mit dem Moped, mit dem Auto und auch zu Fuss.
   Wir haben von Montag bis Freitag Schule. Wir haben Sonnabend frei. Die Schule beginnt um Viertel vor acht, und sie ist um ein Uhr aus.
   Welche Fächer ich habe? Nun, ich habe Deutsch, Mathe, Englisch, Geschichte, Geographie, Sport und Kunst. Ich bin gut in Englisch und in Deutsch. Ich habe eine Eins in Englisch und eine Zwei in Deutsch. Englisch und Deutsch sind leicht. Ich bin nicht so gut in Mathe. Mathe ist schwer. Ich habe nur eine Vier.

2   Übung · Rollenspiel

A classmate plays the role of Gerd. You missed some of his presentation, so you ask him questions about himself. Then you take the role of Gerd, and your classmate asks you.

   A: Wie heisst du?
   B: Ich heisse. . .

3   Übung · Erzähl mal, was Gerd gesagt hat!

A friend of yours missed Gerd's presentation. You tell him or her what Gerd said.

   Der Schüler aus Deutschland heisst. . .

4   Übung · Vortrag   *Presentation*

You are visiting a class in Germany. Tell the class something about yourself and your school day.

5 Schreibübung • Ein Artikel für die Schülerzeitung

The school newspaper in the German school you are visiting would like to write an article about you. Write up the presentation you gave to the class for the school newspaper. Include a picture of yourself.

6 Übung • Immer diese Schule! *School, school, school!*

Practice the following dialogs with a classmate. Try to come up with as many variations as possible and see how long you can keep each conversation going.

1. You talk about how to get to school.
   A: Wie kommst du in die Schule?
   B: Ich komme mit. . .

2. You are in a store and want to know what different school items cost.
   A: Entschuldigung! Was kostet der Kuli?
   B: Er kostet vier Mark.
   A: Danke!
   B: Bitte!

3. You ask your classmate what subjects he or she has on certain days.
   A: Was hast du am Montag?
   B: Ich habe. . .

4. You ask your classmate when he or she has certain subjects.
   A: Wann hast du Deutsch?
   B: Um Viertel vor zehn.

5. You ask your classmates what their grades are in different subjects.
   A: Du, was hast du in Bio?
   B: Ich habe eine Zwei.
   A: Das ist prima!

6. You talk about how easy or difficult certain subjects are.
   A: Mathe ist schwer.
   B: Nein. Mathe ist leicht.

7 Schreibübung • Was passt zusammen? *What goes together?*

Write the pairs.

1. Auf welche Schule gehst du?
2. Wo ist sie?
3. Wie kommst du in die Schule?
4. Was kostet das Wörterbuch?
5. Wie spät ist es?
6. Ich habe um neun Uhr Deutsch.
7. Wann hast du Mathe?
8. Ich habe eine Zwei in Mathe.
9. Du hast eine Eins in Geschichte?
10. Entschuldigung, ist das Herr Meier?

a. Und wann hast du Englisch?
b. Ich habe nur eine Drei.
c. Ja, was hast du?
d. Mit dem Rad.
e. Ja, das ist er.
f. Zwölf Mark sechzig.
g. Um zehn Uhr zwanzig.
h. Es ist acht Uhr.
i. In Westbury.
j. Ich gehe auf die Kennedy-Schule.

Übung • Reklame in der Zeitung   *Ads in the paper*

Look at the following ad and write out what each of the items costs.

Die Bleistifte kosten. . .

10   Aussprache-, Lese- und Schreibübungen

1. Listen carefully and repeat what you hear.

2. Listen, then read aloud.

  1. da, sag, Rad, Tag, schade, Zahl; dem, zehn; wir, prima, sie, wie, vier, sieben, hier, Wien; wo, Montag, Moped; du, Schule, Kuli, Fuss, gut, nur, Uhr
  2. für, grüss, drüben; fünf, München, Niebüll, Glück, Tschüs; blöd, Kröger, Österreich, Wörterbuch
  3. und, sind, Rad, blöd, Deutschland, Sonnabend, Klassenkamerad
  4. sag, Tag, Montag, Dienstag, Donnerstag, Freitag, Samstag, Sonntag, weg
  5. zwanzig, dreissig, vierzig, fünfzig, sechzig

3. Copy the following sentences to prepare yourself to write them from dictation.

  1. Die Zahl sieben.
  2. Um vier Uhr.
  3. Sie sind in Wien.
  4. Mit dem Rad.

Let's review some important points that you have learned in this unit.

Can you say how to get to school?
Using the verb **kommen,** make complete sentences saying how each person comes to school. Vary the means of transportation.
1. Kristin   2. er   3. du   4. Peter und Barbara   5. ich

Can you name some school supplies?
Say the definite article and the plural form of:

Heft, Wörterbuch, Kuli, Bleistift, Schultasche, Taschenrechner, Kassette, Stundenplan

Can you buy things in a store, asking for prices and saying thank you and you're welcome?
Ask how much these items cost and give an answer. Say thank you and you're welcome.

Kuli, Heft, Schultasche, Kassetten

Can you use the right pronoun for people and things?
For each of these nouns, use the pronoun that correctly refers to it:

Schultasche, Lehrer, Mädchen, Taschenrechner, Karin, Bleistifte, Frl. Seifert, Jens, Wörterbuch, Heft

Can you talk about your class schedule?
Say what subjects you have on each day of the week.
Say the names of the days of the week.

Do you know the forms of the verb *haben?*
Write the forms of **haben** that go with these subjects:
1. ich 2. er 3. Sabine und Peter 4. Sabine 5. du
6. Peter 7. sie 8. wir 9. ihr

Can you tell time?
Say what time it is: 7.30; 9.45; 12.50; 1.30; 5.20; 8.15

Can you talk about grades?
What would you say if you got an A? an F?

Can you say whether or not a subject is easy or difficult?
Respond to the following questions:

Du hast eine Eins in Bio? Eine Fünf in Mathe?

WORTSCHATZ

SECTION A
da *there; here*
kommen *to come*
mit dem Auto *by car*
mit dem Bus *by bus*
mit dem Moped *by moped*
mit dem Rad *by bicycle*
mit der Strassenbahn *by streetcar*
schau! *look!*
die **Schule, -n** *school*
toll! *great!*
wie kommst du in die Schule? *how do you get to school?*
zu Fuss *on foot*

SECTION B
bitte *please; you're welcome*
der **Bleistift, -e** *pencil*
da drüben *over there*
danke *thank you, thanks*
DM = Deutsche Mark *German mark*
dort *there*
dort drüben *over there*
du, . . . *hey, . . .*
Entschuldigung! *excuse me!*
er *he; it*
es *it; she*
das **Heft, -e** *notebook*
hier *here*
die **Kassette, -n** *cassette*
der **Kuli, -s** *ballpoint pen*
die **Mark, -** *mark (German monetary unit);* **eine Mark** *one mark*
nicht *not*
nur *only*
das **Poster, -** *poster*
prima! *great!*
schau mal! *look!*
die **Schulsachen** (pl) *school supplies*
die **Schultasche, -n** *schoolbag*
sie *she; it; they*
der **Stundenplan, ̈e** *class schedule*

der **Taschenrechner, -** *pocket calculator*
Unsinn! *nonsense!*
die **Verkäuferin** *salesperson*
was? *what?*
was kosten? *how much are?*
was kostet? *how much is?*
weg *gone*
weiss: ich weiss nicht *I don't know*
wo? *where?*
das **Wörterbuch, ̈er** *dictionary*

SECTION C
am Freitag *on Friday*
aus *out, over*
beginnt *begins*
Bio *short for* Biologie
Biologie *biology*
dann *then*
Deutsch *German*
der **Dienstag** *Tuesday*
der **Donnerstag** *Thursday*
ein, eine *a, an*
Englisch *English*
das **Fach, ̈er** *subject*
frei *off;* **er hat frei** *he has off, he has no school*
der **Freitag** *Friday*
gehen: sie gehen in die neunte Klasse *they're in the ninth grade*
Geographie *geography*
Geschichte *history*
haben *to have*
halb: halb zehn *nine thirty*
heute *today*
ihr *you (pl)*
in *in*
jetzt *now*
die **Klasse, -n** *class; grade*
die **Klassenarbeit, -en** *test*
der **Klassenkamerad, -en** *classmate*
Kunst *art*
Latein *Latin*
Mathe *math*
der **Mittwoch** *Wednesday*

Moment mal! *wait a minute!*
der **Montag** *Monday*
Musik *music*
na *well*
nach *after, past*
der **Name, -n** *name*
die **Oberschule, -n** *high school;* **er geht auf die Oberschule** *he goes to high school*
die **Parallelklasse, -n** *class of the same grade*
die **Pause, -n** *break, recess*
Physik *physics*
Religion *religion*
der **Sonnabend** *Saturday*
sonnabends *(on) Saturdays*
spät: wie spät ist es? *what time is it? (see page 75)*
um *at;* **um acht Uhr** *at eight o'clock;* **um eins** *at one*
viel Glück! *good luck!*
Viertel nach neun *a quarter after nine*
vor *before, of*
wann? *when?*
welche? *which, what?*
wir *we*
die **Zahlen von 5 bis 60** *the numbers from 5 to 60 (p. 74)*
die **Zeit** *time*

SECTION D
aber *but*
Algebra *algebra*
blöd *stupid, dumb*
eine **Eins** *a one (see page 79)*
gut *good*
die **Hausaufgaben** (pl) *homework*
leicht *easy*
macht: er macht Mathe *he's doing math*
die **Note, -n** *grade, mark*
phantastisch *fantastic, great*
schade! *too bad!*
schlecht *bad*
schwer *difficult*
so *so*

WORTSCHATZÜBUNGEN

1. Look at the nouns in the **Wortschatz** above and note how the plural forms are indicated. Then write out each noun in the plural.
2. Make a list of all the words that are similar to English, writing both the German and the English. Compare the spelling and meaning of the words in each pair.

ZUM LESEN

Hausaufgabenlied 📼

Endlich° ist die Schule aus,
und ich gehe jetzt nach Haus',
pack' alles aus der Tasche aus.

Bleistift, Kuli und Papier,
Hefte, Bücher—zwei, drei, vier.
Taschenrechner? Ja, alles hier.

Mathe, Deutsch, Biologie,
Englisch, Kunst, Geographie,
Latein, Geschichte und Chemie.

Hausaufgaben muss ich machen°,
Hausaufgaben, nichts zu lachen°!
Hausaufgaben—viel° zu schwer!
Hausaufgaben—danke sehr°!

Übung • Beantworte die Fragen!

1. Was ist aus?
2. Wohin geht der Schüler?
3. Was macht er?
4. Was packt er aus der Tasche?

5. Welche Fächer hat er?
6. Was macht er jetzt?
7. Sind die Hausaufgaben leicht?

Hausaufgabenlied *homework song*   **endlich** *finally*   **muss ich machen** *I have to do*   **nichts zu lachen** *no laughing matter*   **viel** *much*   **danke sehr** *thank you very much—you can have them*

Übung • Stimmt oder stimmt nicht?

According to Paul's dream, are these statements true or not true?

1. Es ist Montag.
2. Paul kommt zu spät in die Schule.
3. Paul kommt mit dem Bus in die Schule.
4. Pauls Freunde kommen auch zu spät.
5. Paul hat die Hausaufgaben.
6. Was?! Es ist Sonnabend.

---

der Traum *dream* **schnell!** *hurry up!* **ich komme zu spät** *I'll be late* **warten!** *wait!* **endlich** *finally* **zu Hause** *at home* **Gott sei Dank!** *Thank heavens!* **Sonntag** *Sunday*

KAPITEL 3
Freizeit

Young people in German-speaking countries like to do many of the same things you do in your free time. Their free time, however, is often limited. Many teenagers are in apprenticeship programs. They work full-time most of the week and attend trade school one or two days. Young people who attend high school are required to put a great deal of time into their studies.

In this unit you will:

SECTION A	talk about your favorite sports and activities
SECTION B	say when and how often you do these activities
SECTION C	express an opinion, agree or disagree, and say what you like, dislike, or prefer
TRY YOUR SKILLS	use what you've learned
ZUM LESEN	read for practice and pleasure

What do young Germans do in their free time? They participate in sports, play games, and have hobbies. They enjoy music and like to get together with their friends. How do you spend your free time?

A1   Freizeit: Sport und Hobbys 📼

INTERVIEWER	Wie heisst du?
JENS	Ich heisse Jens.
INTERVIEWER	Wie alt bist du?
JENS	Sechzehn.
INTERVIEWER	Was machst du in deiner Freizeit?
JENS	Tja, ich besuche Freunde, ich höre Musikkassetten, ich. . .

Jens besucht Freunde. Sie hören Musikkassetten.

INTERVIEWER	Machst du Sport?
JENS	Ja. Ich schwimme, und ich spiele Tennis.

Jens schwimmt, und er spielt Tennis.

INTERVIEWER	Spielst du auch Fussball?
JENS	Na klar!

Jens spielt auch Fussball.

INTERVIEWER	Spielst du ein Instrument?
JENS	Ja, ich spiele Gitarre.

Er spielt Gitarre.

Jens sammelt Briefmarken.

INTERVIEWER	Hast du auch Hobbys?
JENS	Ich sammle Briefmarken, und ich spiele Schach.

Übung • Mix-Match: Was macht Jens?

1. Jens besucht . . .	Briefmarken.
2. Er hört . . .	Freunde.
3. Jens spielt auch . . .	Musikkassetten.
4. Und er . . .	schwimmt.
5. Er sammelt . . .	Tennis.

A3 Übung • Bilder-Quiz: Was macht Jens? Er . . .

1.  2.  3.  4.  5.

A4 ERKLÄRUNG
Addressing Someone Using the du-form

When you talk to a friend in German, use **du** with the verb form ending in **-st: du bist, du hast, du spielst.** When someone addresses you, respond using **ich** with the verb form ending in **-e: ich habe, ich spiele.** The form **ich bin** is an exception.

du-*form*	**ich**-*form*
Wie **heisst du?**	**Ich heisse** Jens.
Wie alt **bist du?**	**Ich bin** fünfzehn.
Hast du Hobbys?	Ja, **ich habe** auch Hobbys.
Spielst du Tennis?	Nein, **ich spiele** Fussball.
Sammelst du Briefmarken?	Ja, **ich sammle** Briefmarken.

A5 Übung • Jetzt bist du dran

The interviewer asks and you answer yes to all the questions.

    A: Machst du Sport?
    B: Ja, ich mache Sport.

1. Spielst du Gitarre?   3. Sammelst du Briefmarken?   5. Hörst du Musikkassetten?
2. Hast du Hobbys?   4. Besuchst du Freunde?   6. Schwimmst du auch?

A6 Übung • Frag deinen Mitschüler!

Ask your classmate if he or she has the same interests as Jens does.

    A: Jens spielt Schach.
    B: Spielst du auch Schach?

1. Jens besucht Freunde.   3. Jens sammelt Briefmarken.   5. Jens schwimmt.
2. Jens hat Musikkassetten.   4. Jens spielt Fussball.   6. Jens spielt Gitarre.

A7   WIE SAGT MAN DAS?
Asking about someone's interests

Here are some phrases that you can use to ask a friend about his or her interests.

Was machst du?	What are you doing?
Was machst du in deiner Freizeit?	What do you do in your spare time?
Machst du Sport?	Do you participate in sports?
Spielst du Fussball?	Do you play soccer?
Hast du Hobbys?	Do you have hobbies?

A8   Übung • Partnerarbeit

Now ask your classmates what they do in their spare time.
Then have a classmate ask you.

    A: Was machst du in deiner Freizeit?
    B: Ich . . .

1.

2.

3.

4.

5.

6.

7.

8.

Neu im Sport

Drachenfliegen, Eistanzen, Gymnastik, Aerobics und Windsurfen sind heute sehr populär.

1.

2.

3.

4.

5.

A 10 Übung • Und du? Wie steht's mit dir?

1. Was machst du in deiner Freizeit?
2. Machst du Sport?

3. Spielst du auch Tennis?
4. Hast du Hobbys?

INTERVIEWER Und was macht ihr? Macht ihr auch Sport?
GÜNTER Wir spielen Basketball.

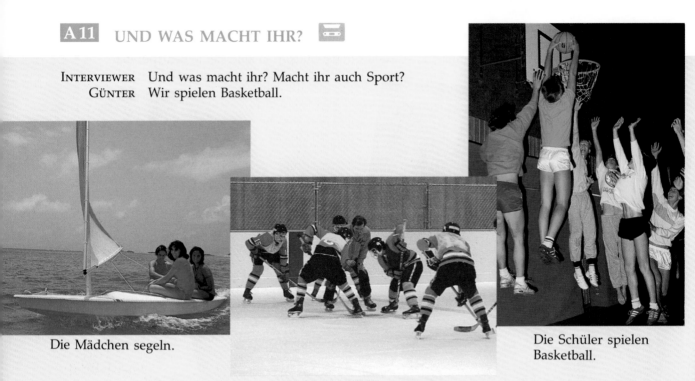

Die Mädchen segeln.

Die Jungen spielen Hockey.

Die Schüler spielen Basketball.

Günter und Kurt sammeln Münzen.

INTERVIEWER Habt ihr Hobbys?
GÜNTER Ja, ich sammle Münzen.
INTERVIEWER Und du, Kurt?
KURT Ich auch.

Die vier Klassenkameraden spielen Karten.
Das Spiel heisst Mau-Mau.

INTERVIEWER Was spielt ihr?
KRISTIN Mau-Mau[1].
INTERVIEWER Wirklich? Wer gewinnt?
KRISTIN Der Jens und der Jörg.
JENS Wie immer.
KRISTIN Aber ihr mogelt. Wie immer.
JENS Was?! Wir mogeln nicht. Ihr
verliert, und ihr seid sauer.
Haha!

[1]**Mau-Mau** is a card game similar to crazy eights.

Übung • Mix-Match: Was machen die Jungen und Mädchen?

1. Günter und Kurt . . .	das Spiel?
2. Sie sammeln auch . . .	die Jungen?
3. Die Mädchen . . .	gewinnen.
4. Die Jungen . . .	Mau-Mau.
5. Die vier Klassenkameraden . . .	Münzen.
6. Das Spiel heisst . . .	nicht.
7. Wer gewinnt . . .	segeln.
8. Jens und Jörg . . .	spielen Basketball.
9. Mogeln . . .	spielen Hockey.
10. Nein, sie mogeln . . .	spielen Karten.

A 13 Übung • Bilder-Quiz: Was machen die Jungen und Mädchen?

Sie segeln.   Sie . . .

1.

2.

3.

4.

5.

6.

7.

8.

A 14 Übung • Der Sport- und Hobbymuffel!

Nein, ich segle nicht.

This boy doesn't do anything! When you ask him if he does the activities pictured in A13, he always answers no!

Segelst du? Nein, ich segle nicht.
Spielst du . . .?

A 15 ERKLÄRUNG
Addressing People Using the ihr-*form*

When you talk to two friends in German, use **ihr** with the verb form ending in **-t: ihr macht, ihr spielt, ihr habt.** When you answer for yourself and somebody else, use **wir** and the verb form ending in **-en** or only in **-n.** The forms **ihr seid** and **wir sind** are exceptions.

ihr-*form*	wir-*form*
Was **macht ihr?**	**Wir machen** Sport.
Habt ihr Hobbys?	Ja, **wir haben** Hobbys.
Spielt ihr Tennis?	**Wir spielen** Fussball.
Segelt ihr?	Ja, **wir segeln.**
Seid ihr sauer?	Ja, **wir sind** sauer.

A 16 Übung • Interview

The interviewer is asking you and your friends what you do. You speak for everyone and answer yes.

A: Macht ihr Sport?
B: Ja, wir machen Sport.

1. Spielt ihr Basketball?
2. Segelt ihr?
3. Sammelt ihr Münzen?

4. Spielt ihr Schach?
5. Verliert ihr?
6. Seid ihr sauer?

A 17 Übung • Was macht ihr?

The interviewer is surprised at your answers. What does he say?

A: Wir spielen Karten.
B: Wirklich? Ihr spielt Karten?

1. Wir spielen Basketball.
2. Wir spielen Gitarre.
3. Wir sammeln Münzen.

4. Wir spielen Mau-Mau.
5. Wir gewinnen.
6. Wir sind sauer.

Basketball ist nicht mein Sport.

A 18 Übung • Lücken-Dialog

Practice the following dialog with a classmate, supplying the missing words.

Was . . . ihr?

Wir . . . Mau-Mau.

Wirklich? Wer . . . das Spiel?

Die Uschi. Aber sie . . .

Die Uschi . . . nicht. Du . . .,
und du . . . sauer.

ERKLÄRUNG
The Present Tense

1. The statements and questions that you have been practicing all refer to present time. Therefore, the verbs in these statements and questions are in the present tense.

Was **machst** du?   Ich **spiele** Tennis.

2. Present tense verb forms have endings. The ending you use depends upon the noun (**Jens, Ursel, Jens und Ursel**) or the pronoun (**ich, du, er, sie, es, wir, ihr, sie**) used with the verb.

3. The following chart summarizes the different verb forms, using **spielen** as a model.

	Singular			*Plural*	
Ich	spiel**e**		Wir	spiel**en**	
Du	spiel**st**	Tennis.	Ihr	spiel**t**	Tennis.
Jens (er)	spiel**t**		Jens und	spiel**en**	
Ursel (sie)	spiel**t**		Ursel (sie)		

4. When speaking to adults such as your teacher, salespeople, or any adults who are not family members or relatives, you must use the formal form of address: **Sie. Sie** is used with the verb form ending in **-en,** the same verb form used with **wir** and **sie** (plural).

Wie **heissen Sie?**   Was **machen Sie?**
Woher **sind Sie,** Herr Huber?   **Spielen Sie** Tennis?

5. All verbs have a base form, the form appearing in your word list **(Wortschatz)** or in a dictionary. This form is called the infinitive. The infinitive of most German verbs has the ending **-en,** as in **spielen,** *to play.* Some verbs end in **-n,** such as **segeln,** *to sail,* **mogeln,** *to cheat,* **sammeln,** *to collect.* The **ich**-form of these verbs is: **ich segle, ich mogle, ich sammle.**

A 20 Übung • Bilder-Quiz: Was machen die Schüler?

Say what everyone does, using the words and pictures as cues.

Wir . . .

Jens . . .

Ihr . . .

Ich . . .

Die Mädchen . . .

Du . . .

Die Jungen . . .

Wir . . .

Er . . .

Du . . .?

A 21 Übung • Frag mal deinen Lehrer!

Now ask your teacher about his or her sports and hobbies. Use the following
questions and the pictures in A20 as a guide.

    1. Was . . . Sie?   **2.** Spiel- . . .?

A 22 Übung • Versteckte Sätze *Hidden sentences*

Look for sentences. How many can you make?

Ich spiele Karten.

ich	besuchen	das Spiel
du	hört	Freunde
Jens	ist	immer
wir	mogelt	Karten
ihr	sammelst	Münzen
die Jungen	spiele	Musik
Ursel	verlieren	sauer

A 23 Übung • Hör gut zu!

Are you talking to one friend, several friends, or an adult? Listen.

	0	1	2	3	4	5	6	7	8	9	10
addressing one student											
addressing several students	✔										
addressing an adult											

A 24 Schreibübung

1. Rewrite the following questions and statements, supplying the appropriate verb endings.

    1. Was mach___ du? Ich spiel___ Karten.
    2. Was mach___ Jens? Er spiel___ Tennis.
    3. Die Jungen spiel___ Mau-Mau. Mogel___ der Jens?
    4. Mach___ ihr Sport? Ja, wir schwimm___ .
    5. Spiel___ Sie Schach, Herr Huber?

2. You have met two young people and would like to know more about them.
What questions would you ask? Think of at least eight questions and write them
down. Remember to use the **ihr**-form.

Young people pursue sports and activities after school and on the weekend. They take tennis and music lessons, and they belong to sports and computer clubs. When do you have your activities? Do you take any lessons? Do you belong to a club?

B1   Wann machst du Sport? 📼

Was macht ihr im Sommer? Im Herbst? Im Winter? Im Frühjahr?

Ursel: Im Sommer spiele ich Tennis, und ich schwimme.

Peter: Im Herbst spiele ich Fussball.

Hans: Im Winter spiele ich Eishockey, und ich laufe Schi.

Karin: Im Frühjahr spiele ich Basketball.

Jörg, was machst du am Wochenende?

Jörg: Am Wochenende spiele ich Fussball.

JULI	JULI	JULI
7	**13**	**14**
SONNTAG	SONNAB./SAMST.	SONNTAG

am Sonntag   am Wochenende

B2 Übung • Und du? Wie steht's mit dir?

1. Was machst du im Sommer?
   Ich . . .
2. Was machst du im Winter?
   Ich . . .
3. Was machst du im Frühjahr?
   Ich . . .
4. Was machst du im Herbst?
   Ich . . .

B3 WIE OFT MACHT IHR SPORT?

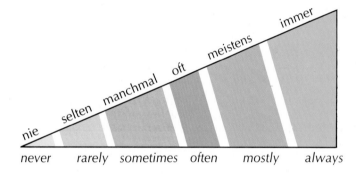

never   rarely   sometimes   often   mostly   always

x	einmal	am Tag
xx	zweimal	in der Woche
xxx	dreimal	im Monat
xxxx	viermal	im Jahr (im Sommer)

PETRA:
„Ich spiele selten Tennis. Ja, manchmal im Sommer. Im Winter spiele ich oft Basketball."

MICHAEL:
„Ich mache Sport viermal in der Woche. Einmal, meistens am Mittwoch, spiele ich Tennis. Am Wochenende spiele ich Fussball, und ich schwimme zweimal in der Woche."

B4 Übung • Was sagt Michael? Was sagt Petra? Erzähl mal!

Report what these students have just told you about how often they have their activities.

1. Michael sagt, er macht . . .   2. Petra sagt, sie spielt . . .

B5 Ein wenig Landeskunde

How much free time do young Germans actually have? Many teenagers are learning a trade and are required to be at work all day. They may have one day a week of classes at a **Berufsschule,** *vocational school.* Their free time is limited to evenings and weekends.

   Teenagers who attend high schools have more free time. The school day is over by 1:00 P.M., and though some states in Germany have school on Saturday twice a month, most do not. Many students belong to **Sportvereine,** *sport clubs,* outside of school. Students have **Sport,** *gym,* as part of the curriculum, but there are few intramural sports and school teams. Musical activities are usually not part of school. There are many orchestras, choirs, and music clubs as well as other types of clubs for people of all ages in the community.

High school students usually do not have part-time jobs, though some may do things like distributing flyers for a local store or babysitting.

B6 ERKLÄRUNG
Word Order: Verb in Second Place

If you listen to what these students are saying, you will notice that most of the statements do not begin with **ich,** but with some other phrase, such as **im Sommer, am Wochenende,** etc. The verb, however, always remains in second place.

	Verb in second place		
Ich	**spiele**	am Wochenende	Fussball.
Am Wochenende	**spiele**	ich	Fussball.
Ich	**spiele**	im Winter	Basketball.
Im Winter	**spiele**	ich	Basketball.

B7 Übung • Frag deine Mitschüler! Frag deinen Lehrer!

Ask your classmates what they do in various seasons of the year and on various days of the week. Ask them how often they do their sports and hobbies. First ask one classmate, then ask a few at once, and then ask your teacher.

A: Was machst du im Winter?
B: Im Winter . . .

A: Was machst du am Wochenende?
B: Am Wochenende . . .

A: Wie oft machst du Sport?
B: Zweimal in der Woche . . .

A: Wie oft spielst du Tennis?
B: Tennis . . .

B8 Übung • Hör gut zu!

When or how often? Listen.

	0	1	2	3	4	5	6	7	8	9	10
wann											
wie oft?											

B9 Schreibübung • Sport ist prima!

Rewrite the following paragraph, varying word order.

Sport ist prima! Ich spiele am Dienstag und am Freitag Tennis. Ich spiele am Samstag Fussball. Ich spiele auch Fussball im Sommer. Fussball ist toll! Wir sind gut. Wir gewinnen meistens; wir verlieren selten. Ich laufe im Winter Schi, und ich spiele Hockey. Ich habe einmal in der Woche Musik. Ich spiele Gitarre. Ich besuche oft Freunde, und wir hören Kassetten. Das ist auch toll!

Young people like to sit around and discuss their opinions and talk about their interests. What do you like to do? What are your favorite activities?

C1   Fussball ist Klasse! 📼

INTERVIEWER   Was machst du, Margit?
               Machst du Sport?
MARGIT   Ich mache Gymnastik.
INTERVIEWER   Wirklich?
MARGIT   Ja, Gymnastik macht Spass!

INTERVIEWER   Jörg, du spielst Fussball?
JÖRG   Ja, Fussball ist Klasse.
INTERVIEWER   Spielst du auch Tennis?
JÖRG   Nein. Ich finde Tennis langweilig.

INTERVIEWER   Wiebke, was machst du in deiner Freizeit?
WIEBKE   Ich lese viel.
INTERVIEWER   Das ist interessant. Was liest du?
WIEBKE   Romane, Sportbücher, Fantasy-Bücher . . .
             sie sind Spitze!
INTERVIEWER   Wie findest du Comics?
WIEBKE   Blöd!

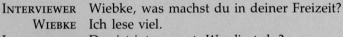

Übung • Mix-Match: Was machen die drei Schüler?

Romane.
Gymnastik.
ist Klasse.
langweilig.
lese viel.
sind blöd.
Spass.
Tennis.

1. Die Margit macht . . .
2. Das macht . . .
3. Der Jörg sagt, Fussball . . .
4. Er spielt nicht . . .
5. Er findet Tennis . . .
6. Wiebke sagt: Ich . . .
7. Ich lese . . .
8. Die Comics . . .

C3   WIE SAGT MAN DAS?
Asking for an opinion, expressing enthusiasm or lack of it

You already know some expressions for good news **(Das ist gut, prima, phantastisch, toll!)** and for bad news **(Das ist blöd!).** You can also use them to express your opinion about activities you like and dislike. Here are some more words and expressions.

asking for an opinion	Wie findest du Fussball?	What do you think of soccer?
expressing enthusiasm	Ich finde Fussball interessant! Fussball ist Klasse! Das ist Spitze! Fussball macht Spass!	I think soccer is interesting! Soccer is terrific! That's great! Soccer is fun!
lack of enthusiasm	Ich finde Fussball blöd. Fussball ist langweilig.	I think soccer is dumb. Soccer is boring.

C4   Übung • Was meint dein Freund?   *What does your friend think?*

You tell your friend what you think and he or she agrees.

A: Hockey ist toll!
B: Ich finde Hockey auch toll!

1. Fussball ist Spitze.
2. Tennis ist Klasse.
3. Sammeln ist interessant.
4. Kartenspielen ist blöd.
5. Mau-Mau ist langweilig.
6. Gymnastik ist prima.

C5   Übung • Jetzt bist du dran

Ask your classmates how they like the sports and activities shown below.

A: Wie findest du . . . *or* Wie findet ihr . . . ?
B: Ich finde Fussball . . . *or* Fussball ist . . .

Mau-Mau **Fussball** *Hockey* Tennis Segeln
Lesen **Briefmarkensammeln** **Sport** Schach *Musik*
Basketball **Gymnastik** Kartenspielen Schwimmen

Spitze!
super!
Klasse!
toll!
prima!
phantastisch!
interessant!
macht Spass!

langweilig!
blöd!

A: Fussball ist Klasse!
B: Stimmt!

A: Wie findest du die Kassette?
B: Super! Sie ist Spitze!
A: Wirklich? Ich finde sie blöd.

A: Du sammelst Briefmarken?
B: Ja. Sammeln macht Spass.
A: Was? Das finde ich nicht.

A: Kartenspielen ist langweilig.
B: Das finde ich auch.

A: Segeln ist auch langweilig.
B: Stimmt nicht! Segeln ist prima!

C7 WIE SAGT MAN DAS?
Expressing surprise, agreement, disagreement

surprise	Was? Wirklich?	What? Really?
agreement	Stimmt! Das finde ich auch.	True! That's right! I think so, too.
disagreement	Stimmt nicht! Das finde ich nicht.	Not true! That's not so. I don't think so.

C8 Übung • Partnerarbeit

Team up with a classmate. Express an opinion about some sport or activity. Your classmate should agree with your opinion or express surprise and disagree. Then reverse roles.

A: Kartenspielen ist langweilig.
B: Stimmt! *or* Das finde ich auch.

A: Ich finde Hockey prima.
B: Wirklich? Das finde ich nicht.

Übung • Und du? Wie steht's mit dir?

Agree or disagree with the following statements.

1. Segeln ist Klasse!
2. Kartenspielen ist langweilig.
3. Deutsch ist interessant.
4. Eine Zwei in Deutsch ist prima.

5. Wir haben am Samstag Schule.
6. Die Hausaufgaben sind leicht.
7. Briefmarkensammeln ist blöd!
8. Comics sind Spitze!

C10 WAS MACHST DU GERN?

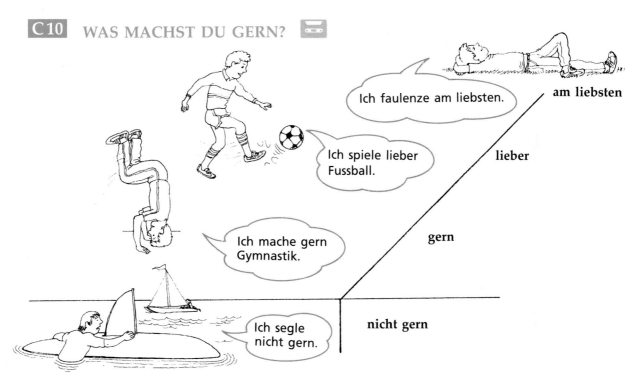

C11 WIE SAGT MAN DAS?
Expressing likes, dislikes, and preferences

Use the word **gern** together with a verb to express the idea of liking something and **nicht gern** to express disliking something.

liking	Ich spiele **gern** Karten.	I like to play cards.
disliking	Ich spiele **nicht gern** Karten.	I don't like to play cards.

Use the word **lieber** together with a verb to express preference. Use **am liebsten** to express what you like best of all.

preference	Ich spiele **lieber** Fussball.	I prefer playing soccer.
strong preference	Ich spiele **am liebsten** Tennis.	I like tennis best of all.

C12 Übung • Und du? Wie steht's mit dir?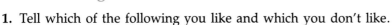

1. Tell which of the following you like and which you don't like.

    Ich spiele gern Tennis.
    Ich . . . gern . . .

    Ich spiele nicht gern Schach.
    Ich . . . nicht gern . . .

2. Tell what you prefer.

    Ich lese nicht gern Comics. Ich lese lieber . . .

3. Now tell what you like to do best of all.

    Ich mache am liebsten . . .

4. Ask your classmates what they like and what they don't like to do. Ask them what they prefer and what they like most of all.

Schach Fussball
Münzen
Romane Bücher
Tennis
Hobbybücher
Gymnastik
Sport Comics
Briefmarken
Mau-Mau

C13 Übung • Der Sport- und Hobbyfreund: Was macht er denn alles?

C14 Übung • Hör gut zu!

Do you like this activity or don't you? What do you prefer?
What do you like best of all? Listen.

	0	1	2	3	4	5	6	7	8	9	10
likes											
does not like											
prefers	✔										
likes most of all											

C15   Schreibübung · Was machen die Schüler gern? Und du?

1. Write what each student likes and doesn't like to do. Use the following cues.

	gern	am liebsten	nicht gern
1. Paul:	Gymnastik	schwimmen	Basketball
2. Sabine:	Karten	Mau-Mau	Schach
3. Monika und Anke:	Kassetten	Sport	sammeln

1. Paul macht gern Gymnastik. Er . . .   2. Sabine . . .

2. Write a paragraph about what you like and don't like to do.

C16   Übung · Umfrage: Was machst du in deiner Freizeit?

The survey sheet below was given to a German 9th-grade class. The students were asked to rank their sports activities, putting their favorite sport at the top of the list. Read the survey sheet and discuss it in class. Tell what this student likes and dislikes, what he prefers, and when and how often he does the various activities listed.

Name: *Markus Walden*

	Was?	im Frühjahr	im Sommer	im Herbst	im Winter	am Wochenende	nie	selten	manchmal	oft	immer	am Tag	in der Woche	im Monat	im Jahr
am liebsten	Fussball	✓	✓			✓				✓			2x		
	Basketball	✓			✓						✓		1x		
lieber	Windsurfen		✓			✓			✓						4x
	Segeln		✓	✓					✓						1x
gern	Volleyball	✓								✓			1x		
	Gymnastik				✓					✓			3x		
nicht gern	Handball				✓			✓					1x		
	Golf			✓				✓							1x

Headers: Was? · Wann? · Wie oft?

C17   Übung · Klassenprojekt

Do a similar survey in your class and discuss the results.

Friends do not always have the same opinion about sports and activities.

1 Stimmt nicht! Du bist nur sauer!

HELMUT Hast du ein Hobby?
JENS Ja, Schach.
HELMUT Was? Schach ist so langweilig.
JENS Das finde ich nicht. Schach ist interessant. Es macht Spass! Spielst du auch Schach?

HELMUT Ja, aber nicht oft.
JENS Bist du gut? Gewinnst du oft?
HELMUT Nein, ich verliere meistens.
JENS Ach so! Du verlierst immer, und du bist sauer.

Aber Lars, Jörg und Jens spielen gern Schach.

2 Übung • Deine Meinung—meine Meinung *Your opinion—my opinion*

Ask a classmate to tell you five things that he or she likes to do. After each response, give your own opinion. If you like the same thing, say why. If you don't like it, say that you prefer something else. Your conversation might go like this:

A: Was machst du gern?
B: Ich spiele gern Hockey.
A: Ich auch. Hockey ist toll! *or* Ich nicht. Ich laufe lieber Schi.

3 Übung • Stimmt!—Stimmt nicht!

Some of your classmates have definite opinions when it comes to certain sports and activities. Listen to what they say and agree or disagree. One classmate might begin by saying:

A: Ach, Hockey ist so langweilig!
B: Das finde ich nicht. *or* Stimmt!

The following are pictorial symbols you can see in stadiums where sports events take place.

1. Identify each symbol:
   1. Fussball
   2. . . .

1.   2.   3.   4.

5.   6.   7.   8.

2. Look at the activities depicted and answer these questions.
   Was machst du gern?
   Was machst du nicht gern?
   Was machst du am liebsten?

3. Now give an opinion on each of the activities shown.
   Ich finde . . .

5   Übung • Wann spielen sie was?

These German friends participate in different sports during different seasons.
According to the diagram, who does what, and when?

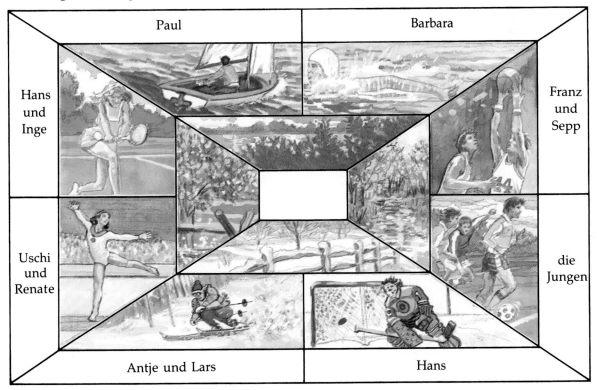

Übung • Hallo! Wer schreibt uns?

The following excerpts are from a special report, „Hallo! Wer schreibt uns?
Wir antworten!", which appeared in a magazine for young people. Report to a
classmate or to your teacher what these two ads say. Use complete sentences.

Vorname: Bettina
Nachname: Schilling
Alter: 14
Strasse: Schulstrasse 17
Stadt: D - 7900 Ulm
Hobbys/Interessen: schwimmen,
    segeln, Basketball spielen

Vorname: Markus
Nachname: Wallner
Alter: 15
Strasse: Hebbelstrasse 8
Stadt: D - 6100 Darmstadt
Hobbys/Interessen: Fussball, Gym-
    nastik, Briefmarken sammeln

7 Schreibübung • Interview und Anzeige

1. Pretend that you would like to place a similar ad in this magazine in order to
   find a pen pal, and you are giving information about yourself over the phone.

   INTERVIEWER   Wie heisst du?
   DU   . . .

2. Write down the phone conversation you had with a person from this magazine.

3. Write how your ad would appear in the column.

8 Übung • Ein Brief an Markus Wallner

Here is a letter that was written in response to Markus Wallner's ad. Read the letter.

Lieber Markus!
    Ich heisse Martin Obermeyer. Ich bin 14 Jahre alt
und wohne in Regensburg (D- 8400) Bahnhofstasse 17.
Meine Interessen sind Musik und Sport. Ich
höre gern Musikgruppen aus England. Ich schwimme
gern, ich spiele Squash, und am liebsten spiele
ich Fussball.
    Was machst Du? Bitte schreib mir!
                              Dein
                              Martin

9 Schreibübung • Jetzt bist du dran

Now write a letter of your own, similar to the one on the preceding page.
Answer either Markus Wallner's ad or Bettina Schilling's.

10 Schreibübung • Klassenprojekt

After your class has written ads to appear in the pen-pal column „Hallo!
Wer schreibt uns?", exchange ads with another German class. Pick a pen
pal and write a letter in response to the ad.

11 Übung • Dialog-Mischmasch

With the help of a classmate, unscramble the following dialog.
Start with 1. Write down your dialog and read it aloud together.

Bist du gut? Gewinnst du oft?

Ach, ich verliere oft.

Na klar! Ich spiele Tennis.

1. Machst du Sport?

Ich gewinne meistens. Und du?

Tennis? Ich finde Tennis langweilig.

Soso. Du bist nur sauer.

Wirklich? Ich spiele gern,
und ich finde Tennis Spitze.

12 Aussprache-, Lese- und Schreibübungen

1. Listen carefully and repeat what you hear.

2. Listen, then read aloud.
   1. frei, Frau, Freund, drei, dreimal, prima, hören, Karte, Roman, Rad
   2. ihr, vier, hier, wir, er, der, schwer
   3. aber, oder, lieber, immer, Sommer, Winter, sauer, Schüler, Lehrer, super
   4. ein, eine, eins, einmal, heisse, Latein
   5. Mau-Mau, sauer, schau, aus, auch
   6. neun, heute, Freund, neunzehn; Fräulein, Verkäuferin
   7. Schule, Schi, schwer, schlecht
   8. spielen, Sport, Spitze, spät; Stundenplan, Bleistift

3. Copy the following sentences to prepare yourself to write them from dictation.
   1. Wir haben immer frei.
   2. Fräulein Meier spielt heute.
   3. Meine Freundin heisst Winter.
   4. Die Schule ist schwer.

WAS KANNST DU SCHON?

Let's review some important points that you have learned in this unit.

SECTION A

Can you address a person using the *du*-form?
Ask a friend questions about his or her interests using the following verbs:
    machen, spielen, sammeln, schwimmen, besuchen

Give a reply for each question.

Can you address a group of people using the *ihr*-form?
Approach a group of people and ask them what they are doing. Give an appropriate response.

Do you know how to address adults?
Ask your teacher about his or her activities.

SECTION B

Can you say when and how often you do various sports and activities?
Mention four activities. Tell when you do them (in what season or on what day) and how often.

Mention activities that you rarely or never do, as well as ones you do sometimes, often, and always.

SECTION C

Can you ask about someone's interests?
Ask a friend what he or she thinks of the following:
    Tennis, Fussball, Gymnastik, Kartenspielen, Briefmarkensammeln

Do you know how to express enthusiasm or lack of enthusiasm?
Give your opinion about five different sports and activities.

Can you express surprise and also say that you agree or disagree with something?
Respond to each of the following statements, expressing surprise, agreement or disagreement.

1. Deutsch ist leicht.
2. Schach ist interessant.
3. Comics sind super.
4. Tennis ist schwer.
5. Briefmarkensammeln ist blöd.

Can you talk about your likes, dislikes, and preferences?
Tell what you like to do, what you prefer to do, and what you like to do most of all. Tell what you don't like to do.

Now ask a friend about his or her likes and dislikes.

WORTSCHATZ

SECTION A

auch: ich auch *me too*
Basketball *basketball*
besuchen *to visit*
die Briefmarke, -n *stamp*
ein *a, an*
die Freizeit *free time; in deiner Freizeit in your free time*
der Freund, -e *friend*
Fussball *soccer*
gewinnen *to win*
die Gitarre, -n *guitar*
haha! *ha ha!*
das Hobby, -s *hobby*
Hockey *hockey*
hören *to listen (to)*
das Instrument, -e *instrument*
der Interviewer, - *interviewer*
die Karten (pl) *cards*
machen *to do; was machst du? what are you doing? what do you do?*
Mau-Mau (card game similar to crazy eights)
mogeln *to cheat*
die Münze, -n *coin*
die Musikkassette, -n *music cassette*
na klar! *of course!*
sammeln *to collect*
sauer *sore*
Schach *chess*
der Schüler, - *student, pupil*
schwimmen *to swim*
segeln *to sail*
Sie *you (formal)*
das Spiel, -e *game*
spielen *to play*
der Sport *sport; sports; Sport machen to participate in a sport, to do sports*

Tennis *tennis*
tja *hm*
verlieren *to lose*
was!? *what!?*
wie immer *as always*
wirklich? *really?*

SECTION B

am Sonntag *on Sunday*
am Tag *(times) a day*
am Wochenende *on the weekend*
dreimal *three times*
einmal *once*
Eishockey *ice hockey*
im Frühjahr *in the spring*
im Herbst *in the fall*
im Jahr *(times) a year*
im Monat *(times) a month*
im Sommer *in the summer*
im Winter *in the winter*
immer *always*
in der Woche *(times) a week*
manchmal *sometimes*
meistens *mostly*
nie *never*
oft *often*
Samstag *Saturday*
Schi: ich laufe Schi *I go skiing*
selten *seldom*
Sonntag *Sunday*
viermal *four times*
wie oft? *how often?*
zweimal *twice*

SECTION C

am liebsten (machen) *to like (to do) most of all*
Comics (pl) *comics*

das Fantasy-Buch, ¨er *fantasy book*
faulenzen *to lie around, be lazy*
finden *to find, think (have the opinion about something); das finde ich nicht I don't think so; wie findest du . . .? how do you like . . .? what do you think of . . .?*
gern (machen) *to like (to do)*
Gymnastik *gymnastics; Gymnastik machen to do gymnastics*
interessant *interesting*
Kartenspielen *playing cards*
Klasse! *great!*
langweilig *boring*
lesen *to read*
lieber (machen) *to prefer (to do); ich spiele lieber Fussball I'd rather play soccer*
liest: was liest du? *what do you read?*
nicht gern (machen) *to not like (to do)*
der Roman, -e *novel*
Sammeln *collecting*
Segeln *sailing*
Spass *fun; Gymnastik macht Spass gymnastics are fun*
Spitze! *terrific!*
das Sportbuch, ¨er *book about sports*
stimmt! *that's right! true!*
stimmt nicht! *not true! that's not so!*
super! *super! terrific!*
viel *much, a lot*

WORTSCHATZÜBUNGEN

1. Look at the **Wortschatz** and make a list of all the verbs. What do most verbs end in? (Look at the last two or three letters.) Now put a slash between the verb infinitive stem and the ending.

2. Pick out the words that are listed twice. What is the difference in spelling? What is the difference in meaning?

3. Make a list of all the words that are similar to English, writing them both in German and English. Compare the spelling and the meaning of each pair of words.

ZUM LESEN

Keine Freizeitmuffel!

Was machen Jungen und Mädchen in der Freizeit?—Sie machen Sport, sie gehen ins Kino, ins Konzert, zu Sportveranstaltungen. Sie hören Musik, diskutieren und philosophieren. Was machen sie noch? Fragen wir sie mal!

Lest ihr gern, oder seht ihr nur fern°?

Frage an Jungen und Mädchen: Wie oft lest ihr in Büchern?	1968	1986
—täglich°:	10%	12%
—2–3 mal in der Woche:	19%	21%
—einmal in der Woche:	13%	11%
—gar nicht:	32%	28%

Was lest ihr? Lest ihr auch Bücher, oder seid ihr Büchermuffel?

„Ich lese viel. Ich lese Zeitschriften°, Hobbybücher— am liebsten lese ich Comics."

Zeitschriften

---

seht ihr nur fern *watch T.V.*   täglich *daily*
Zeitschriften *magazines*

deutsche Zeitungen

"Ich lese nicht viel, die Zeitung, ja—und Sportbücher lese ich, Bücher über Tennis und Fussball und so."

"Ich lese gern. Ich lese täglich die Zeitung, ich lese Zeitschriften und Bücher. Am liebsten lese ich Romane—moderne Autoren, wie Böll, Grass, auch Thomas Mann. Ich lese gerade die Buddenbrooks."

Heinrich Böll
(1917–1985)

Thomas Mann
(1875–1955)

moderne Autoren
der deutschen Sprache

Günter Grass
(1927)

Übung • Sprechen wir darüber! *Let's talk about it!*

1. Was machst du in der Freizeit?
2. Was liest du?
3. Wie oft liest du Bücher? Oder bist du ein Büchermuffel?
4. Was liest du gern? Am liebsten?
5. Welche Autoren liest du?
6. Wie heissen einige deutsche Zeitschriften?
7. Wie heissen einige deutsche Zeitungen?
8. Wie heissen einige Autoren?
9. Die *Buddenbrooks* sind von . . .?
10. Und *Der Butt?*

Wie findet ihr Comics?

"Ich lese schon lange° Comics. Am liebsten lese ich amerikanische Superhelden°-Comics. Manchmal lese ich sie im Original."

"Es gibt auch deutsche Comics. Sie sind nicht so gut. Ich finde Matthias Schultheiss und amerikanische Comics toll."

Michael   Kristin

"Viele° Comics sind blöd. Nur Moebius lese ich gern. Ich finde die Frauen° in den meisten° Comics nicht gut. Sie sind immer blöd und hilflos°."

Andrea

"Ich liebe° Comics, und ich sammle Comics-Hefte. Die Zeichner° Mercier und Moebius finde ich sehr gut."

Natalie   Kurt

"Ich lese Comics selten. Mein Interesse ist Kunst. Aber für mich sind Comics auch Kunst. Am liebsten lese ich MAD."

---

lange *for a long time*   **der Superheld** *super hero*   **viele** *many*   **die Frau** *woman*   **die meisten** *most*   **hilflos** *helpless*
lieben *to love*   **der Zeichner** *artist*

Welche° Figuren kennen° die deutschen Jungen und Mädchen?

Max und Moritz

Mickey Mouse

Asterix

Struwwelpeter

von Dr. Heinr. Hoffmann

Übung • Und du? Wie steht's mit dir?

1. Welche Comics kennst du?
2. Welche Zeichner findest du gut?
3. Welche Comics gibt es?

4. Welche Figuren kennst du?
5. Sammelst du Comics-Hefte?

Neue Hobbys

„Mein Hobby ist der Homecomputer. Ich mache Computerspiele , ich spiele ‚Hangman', und jetzt lerne ich Schach. Schach mit dem Computer! Das ist toll, das macht Spass!"

---

welche *which*   **kennen** *to know*

KAPITEL **4**

Aus einer Schülerzeitung

Wiederholungskapitel

Wir sind Schüler aus der 9c in der List Realschule in München. Wir sind diesen Monat in unserer Schülerzeitung, im List-Käfer. Warum? Wir korrespondieren mit englischen und amerikanischen Schülern.

Das sind unsere „Steckbriefe."

1
Name: Natalie Fiedler
Alter: 15 J.
Hobby: Gymnastik, Tanzen,
   Windsurfen, Schwimmen
Lieblingsfächer: Ek[1], Mu, E
Schulweg: Rad

2
Name: Nicolas Kraindl
Alter: 15 J.
Hobby: Squash, Musik
   (Gitarre spielen)
Lieblingsfächer: Mu, E
Schulweg: Strassenbahn

3
Name: Steffi Huber
Alter: 15 J.
Hobby: Gymnastik, Volleyball,
   Schi laufen
Lieblingsfächer: M, G
Schulweg: U-Bahn

4
Name: Michael Strasser
Alter: 16 J.
Hobby: Hockey, Judo, Schach
Lieblingsfächer: Ku, Ch
Schulweg: U-Bahn

5
Name: Monika Schönfeld
Alter: 16 J.
Hobby: Klavier, Schwimmen,
   Windsurfen, Tennis
Lieblingsfächer: Mu, E, D
Schulweg: Rad/zu Fuss

6
Name: Andreas Reichel
Alter: 16 J.
Hobby: Tennis, Fussball,
   Briefmarken
Lieblingsfächer: D, Bio
Schulweg: Moped

7
Name: Marina Welzel
Alter: 16 J.
Hobby: Musik (Klavier),
   Segeln, Schi laufen
Lieblingsfächer: Mu, E, D
Schulweg: zu Fuss

8
Name: Stefan Knötzinger
Alter: 15 J.
Hobby: Schach, Tennis,
   Basketball
Lieblingsfächer: M, E, Ek
Schulweg: Bus

9
Name: Matthias Blick
Alter: 15 J.
Hobby: Fussball, Schwimmen,
   Schi laufen, Münzen
Lieblingsfächer: D, E
Schulweg: Rad

---

[1]Abkürzungen: Ek = Erdkunde; Mu = Musik; E = Englisch; M = Mathematik; G = Geographie; Ku = Kunst; Ch = Chemie; D = Deutsch; Bio = Biologie; **Schi laufen: sie läuft Schi** *she skis*; **U-Bahn: mit der U-Bahn** *by subway*; **Klavier** *piano*

2 Übung • Beantworte die Fragen!

1. In welche Klasse gehen die Schüler?
2. Wie heisst ihre Schule?
3. Warum sind sie in der Schülerzeitung?
4. Wie heissen die Schüler?
5. Lies die neun Steckbriefe!
6. Identifiziere die Schüler! (Sag, wie sie heissen, wie alt sie sind, was für Hobbys sie haben, was ihre Lieblingsfächer sind und wie sie in die Schule kommen!)
7. Wer ist 15 Jahre alt? Wer ist 16?
8. Wer kommt mit dem Rad in die Schule?
9. Wer kommt mit der Strassenbahn? Und mit der U-Bahn?
10. Wie kommen die andern in die Schule?

3 Übung • Jetzt bist du dran

Your German class is going to be featured in the **List-Käfer.** Interview your classmates and write a **Steckbrief** for each one.

4 Schreibübung • Partnerarbeit

You and your partner are going to interview one of the students shown on page 121. Look back through Units 1, 2, and 3 and make a list of questions you could ask the student.

5 Schreibübung • Interview

Pretend that you are interviewing one of the students on page 121. Write out your interview. Then you and your partner take the roles of the interviewer and the student and present it to the class. Your classmates may have other questions to ask.

6 Schreibübung • Ein Freund aus der List-Schule

Now you and your partner take the interview you have written and rewrite it as a newspaper article.

7 Übung • Klassenprojekt

Collect the articles written by your classmates and make a scrapbook or a bulletin board titled **Unsere Freunde aus der List-Schule.**

Ruth Maier   BUCHHANDLUNG AM RATHAUS

STARNBERG • HAUPTSTRASSE 14 • TELEFON 7341

Bücher, Schallplatten, Schreibwaren & Posters

Bücher — und alles für die Schule Ruth Maier hat's!

Schulsachen

Schultaschen	DM 15,00
Taschenrechner	22,00
Kulis	2,10
Hefte	1,20

Wörterbücher

Wörterbuch D/E—E/D nur DM 12,00!

Bleistifte (10 St.) DM 3,50

Poster ab DM 4,00

Musik

Platten	ab DM	7,00
Kassetten	ab	6,80
Video-Kassetten	ab	12,00

Spiele

Computerspiele DM 23,00

Bücher ab DM 6,00

9 Übung • Beantworte die Fragen!

1. Was hat die Buchhandlung am Rathaus alles?
2. Was kostet alles? Was kostet . . .? Was kosten . . .?

10 Schreibübung • In der Buchhandlung

You go into Ruth Maier's bookstore and want to know the prices of four items. Write out a dialog and practice it with a classmate. Don't forget to be polite.

11 Übung • Aus dem List-Käfer

So sehen die Schüler der List-Schule ihre Schulwoche—Und du?
Wie steht's mit dir? Wie siehst du deine Schulwoche?

LANDESKUNDE 1

A Glimpse of the Federal Republic of Germany

Germany lies in the center of Europe. It is about six hundred miles long, bounded by the North Sea to the north and the Alps to the south. From east to west the country is narrow, seldom more than two hundred miles wide. Contained in this area is a surprising variety of landscapes. There are coastal regions and flatlands in northern Germany and gently rolling hills in the central and southwestern part of the country. South of the river Danube is a high plateau that reaches to the majestic Alpine range. It is surprising that in such a highly industrialized country more than half the area is farmland and another third is forest land.

❶ Promenadenkonzert auf der Nordseeinsel Sylt

❷ Kurort Badenweiler im Schwarzwald

❸ Die Zugspitze, Deutschlands höchster Berg, 2 963 m

125

The North

The North abounds in architectural and artistic treasures and is the area of Germany most influenced by the sea. There are several historic Hanseatic cities, including the great port cities of Hamburg, Bremen, Kiel, and Lübeck. The coasts of the Baltic Sea and the North Sea are dotted with fishing villages. Many have become popular summer resorts, but fishing is still an important industry. Inland is a rich agricultural area that supports a thriving dairy industry. There are many towns with red brick buildings that are characteristic of the north, and villages that still have windmills and thatched-roof houses.

Lieber Gast !

Bitte keine Halme (Reêt) rausziehen. Wenn jeder einen Halm nehmen würde, hätte ich bald kein Dach mehr über dem Kopf.

Der Eigentümer

❶ Ausflugsschiffe vor der Insel Helgoland

❷ Nordfriesenhaus mit Reetdach auf der Insel Föhr

❸ Tracht auf der Insel Föhr

❹ Fischerhafen Bensersiel in Ostfriesland

❺ Das Rathaus von Bremen

❻ Lübeck mit Blick auf das Holstentor (1477)

❼ Schaffner vor dem Lübecker Rathaus

❽ Lüneburger Heide: Schäfer mit Hund und Heidschnucken

❾ Hamburg, grösste Stadt der Bundesrepublik

❿ Berlin: Ruine und Neubau der Kaiser-Wilhelm Gedächtniskirche

Central Germany

The central part of Germany is highly diversified in both geography and character. The busy Moselle River flows through Trier, the oldest city in Germany. The famous Rhine River cuts a scenic path through terraced vineyards, past romantic castles and the rock upon which the fabled Lorelei sat, through the great cities of Cologne, Düsseldorf, and Bonn, the capital of the Federal Republic of Germany. The state of North Rhine–Westphalia, its rolling hills sprinkled with old castles, is called the forge of Germany because of its highly industrialized Ruhr area with such cities as Essen and Dortmund. The second largest industrialized area of the Rhine-Main region is Hessia, but it is also known as the land of healing springs because of its many spas. Located in Hessia is the city of Frankfurt, the business and banking capital of the Federal Republic.

❶ Fachwerkhäuser in Paderborn, Westfalen

❷ Der Wormser Dom aus dem 11. und 12. Jahrhundert

❸ Weinberge in Bacharach am Rhein

❹ Trier, die älteste Stadt, mit der Porta Nigra aus der Zeit der Römer

5 Braunkohlenwerk in der Nähe von Jülich, im Rheinland

6 Arbeiter im Ruhrgebiet

7 Der Rhein in der Nähe von Duisburg

8 Frankfurt am Main, Finanzzentrum der Bundesrepublik

The South

The South, a beautiful and historic region, begins at the River Main and stretches all the way to Switzerland, Lake Constance, and the Alps. In this area are found the old university cities of Heidelberg, Tübingen, and Freiburg; historic art cities such as Würzburg, Nürnberg, and Bamberg; perfectly preserved medieval towns such as Rothenburg, Dinkelsbühl, and Nördlingen; wine-growing regions in the southwest; and spas that pre-date Roman times. Munich, the capital of Bavaria, is in the southeast, a center of art and culture, and the city in which sixty-nine percent of all Germans would like to live. The area around Munich offers both natural and man-made wonders, baroque churches, monasteries, and King Ludwig's castles. The Alps themselves offer magnificent scenery, dotted with lakes, forests, flower-filled meadows, and charming Alpine villages that are year-round resorts.

❶ Blumenfrau auf dem Marktplatz in Freiburg

❷ Gasthaus zur Sonne

❸ Schwarzwälder Schinken und Bauernbrot

❹ Heidelberg am Neckar, Universitätsstadt seit 1386

❺ Rathausfassade von Staufen an der Badener Weinstrasse

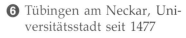

6 Tübingen am Neckar, Universitätsstadt seit 1477

7 Treppenhaus in der Würzburger Residenz mit dem in der Welt grössten Deckenfresko von Tiepolo

8 Das Rathaus von Ulm mit Fresken von 1540

9 Landshut an der Isar, mit Giebelhäusern aus dem 15. und 16. Jahrhundert

1. Insel Mainau im Bodensee

2. Luftkurort und Geigenbauerstadt Mittenwald, am Fusse
   des Karwendelgebirges

3. Die Fuggerei (1519) in Augs-
   burg hat die ältesten Sozial-
   wohnungen der Welt

4. Personenfähre am Tegernsee,
   von Bad Wiessee nach Rottach

5. Lüftlmalerei an einem Haus
   im Festspielort Oberammergau

FOR REFERENCE

SUMMARY OF FUNCTIONS

The term *functions* can be defined as what you do with language—what your purpose is in speaking. As you use this textbook, you will find yourself in a number of situations—in a store, in a restaurant, at a party, at the airport, in a new city. How do you "function" in these situations? How do you ask about prices in a store, order a meal in a restaurant, compliment your host at a party, greet arriving friends at an airport, or ask for directions in an unfamiliar city? You need to know certain basic functional expressions.

Here is a list of functions accompanied by the expressions you have learned to communicate them. The number of the unit in which the expressions were introduced is followed by the section letter and number in parentheses.

SOCIALIZING

Saying hello
1 (A3)   Guten Morgen!
          Guten Tag!
          short forms: Morgen!
                         Tag!
          informal: Hallo!
          regional: Grüss dich!

Saying goodbye
1 (A3)   Auf Wiedersehen!
          short form: Wiedersehen!
          informal: Tschüs!
                      Tschau!
                      Bis dann!

Addressing people
1 (A1)   *first name*

1 (A7)   Herr + *last name*
          Frau + *last name*
          Fräulein + *last name*

3 (A4)   *with* du
  (A15) *with* Ihr
  (A19) *with* Sie

Getting someone's attention
2 (B25) Du, (Jens), . . .
          Schau!
          Schau, (Jens)!
          Schau mal!
          Schau mal, (Jens)!
          Entschuldigung!

Saying please
2 (B8)   Bitte!

Saying thank you
2 (B8)   Danke!

Responding to thank you
2 (B8)   Bitte!

Expressing good wishes
2 (C10) Viel Glück!

Saying you don't understand
1 (D14) Wie bitte?
          Woher?
          Wer?
          Der (Stefan)?
          Ich?

EXCHANGING INFORMATION

Asking someone his or her name
1 (B5)   Wie heisst du?

1 (D16) Wie heissen Sie?

  and giving yours
1 (B5)   Ich heisse . . .

Asking someone else's name
1 (B5)   Wie heisst er / sie?

  and giving it
          Er / sie heisst . . .

Asking who someone is
1 (B9)   Wer ist das?

Identifying people and places
1 (B9)   Das ist . . .

Asking someone his or her age
    1 (C7)   Wie alt bist du?

and giving yours
            Ich bin (15).
            Ich bin (15) Jahre alt.

telling someone else's age
            Er / sie ist (15) Jahre alt.

Asking someone where he or she is from
    1 (D4)   Woher bist du?

and saying where you are from
            Ich bin aus . . .

saying where someone else is from
            Er / sie ist aus . . .

Asking someone about his or her interests
    3 (A7)   Was machst du?
            Machst du (Sport)?
            Spielst du (Fussball)?
            Hast du Hobbys?

Answering questions
    1 (D8)   Ja, . . .
            Nein, . . .

    3 (A1)   Na, klar!

Saying you don't know
    2 (B20)   Ich weiss nicht.

Inquiring about prices
    2 (B16)   Was kostet . . .?

Saying that you don't do something in general or usually
    3 (A14)   Ich (segle) nicht.

    (B3)   Ich (spiele) nie (Fussball).

EXPRESSING ATTITUDES AND OPINIONS

Expressing agreement
    2 (D1)   Ja, . . .
            Ja, das ist (blöd).
    3 (C7)   Stimmt!
            Das finde ich auch.
Expressing disagreement
    3 (C7)   Stimmt nicht!
            Das finde ich nicht.

Contradicting, correcting
    2 (B20)   Unsinn! Das ist . . .

Asking for an opinion
    3 (C3)   Wie findest du . . .?

Giving an opinion
    3 (C3)   Ich finde . . . (toll).

EXPRESSING FEELINGS AND EMOTIONS

Expressing surprise
    3 (C7)   Was?!
            Wirklich?

Expressing liking
    3 (C11)   Ich (spiele) gern (Gitarre).

Expressing dislike
    3 (C11)   Ich (spiele) nicht gern (Fussball).

Expressing preference
    3 (C11)   Ich (spiele) lieber . . .

Expressing strong preference
    3 (C11)   Ich (spiele) am liebsten . . .

Responding to good news
    2 (D5)   Gut!
            Prima!
            Phantastisch!
            Toll!

Responding to bad news
    2 (D5)   Blöd!
            Das ist nicht so gut.
            Das ist schlecht.
            Schade!

Expressing enthusiasm
    2 (A1)   Toll!
    3 (C1)   Ich finde . . . interessant!
            . . . ist Klasse / Spitze / super /
                prima / phantastisch / toll!
            . . . macht Spass!

Expressing lack of enthusiasm
    3 (C1)   Ich finde . . . blöd.
            . . . ist langweilig.

GRAMMAR SUMMARY

DETERMINERS

In German, nouns can be grouped into three classes or genders: masculine, feminine, and neuter. There are words that tell you the gender of a noun. One of these is called the definite article. In English there is one definite article: *the.* In German there are three, one for each gender: **der, die,** and **das.**

Gender:	Masculine	Feminine	Neuter
Noun Phrase:	**der Junge** *the boy* **der Ball** *the ball*	**die Mutter** *the mother* **die Kassette** *the cassette*	**das Mädchen** *the girl* **das Haus** *the house*

DEFINITE ARTICLES

Masculine *Feminine* *Neuter*	**der** **die** **das**
Plural	**die**

NOUN PLURALS

Noun gender and plural forms are not always predictable. Therefore, you must learn each noun together with its article (**der, die, das**) and with its plural form. As you learn more nouns, however, you will discover certain patterns. Although there are always exceptions to these patterns, you may find them helpful in remembering the plural forms of many nouns.

Most German nouns form their plurals in one of five ways. Some nouns add endings in the plural; some add endings and/or change the sound of the stem vowel in the plural, indicating the sound change with the umlaut (¨). Only the vowels **a, o, u** and the diphthong **au** can take the umlaut. If a noun has an umlaut in the singular, it keeps the umlaut in the plural. Most German nouns fit into one of the following plural groups:

Group:	I	II	III	IV	V
Endings:	–	–e	–er	–(e)n	–s
Umlaut:	*sometimes*	*sometimes*	*always*	*never*	*never*

1. Nouns in Group I do not have any ending in the plural. Sometimes they take an umlaut. NOTE: There are only two feminine nouns in this group: **die Mutter** *(mother)* and **die Tochter** *(daughter).*

der Lehrer, die Lehrer
der Schüler, die Schüler
die Mutter, die Mütter
die Tochter, die Töchter

das Fräulein, die Fräulein
das Mädchen, die Mädchen
das Poster, die Poster

2. Nouns in Group II add the ending **-e** in the plural. Sometimes they take an umlaut. NOTE: There are many one-syllable words in this group.

der Bleistift, die Bleistifte   das Jahr, die Jahre
der Freund, die Freunde   das Spiel, die Spiele
der Stundenplan, die Stundenpläne das Stück, die Stücke

3. Nouns in Group III add the ending **-er** in the plural. They always take an umlaut wherever possible, that is when the noun contains the vowels **a, o,** or **u,** or the diphthong **au.** NOTE: There are no feminine nouns in this group. There are many one-syllable words in this group.

das Buch, die Bücher
das Fach, die Fächer
das Land, die Länder

4. Nouns in Group IV add the ending **-en** or **-n** in the plural. They never add an umlaut. NOTE: There are many feminine nouns in this group.

der Herr, die Herren   der Kamerad, die Kameraden
der Junge, die Jungen   der Name, die Namen
die Frau, die Frauen   die Zahl, die Zahlen
die Karte, die Karten
die Klasse, die Klassen

Feminine nouns ending in **-in** add the ending **-nen** in the plural.

die Freundin, die Freundinnen
die Lehrerin, die Lehrerinnen

5. Nouns in Group V add the ending **-s** in the plural. They never add an umlaut. NOTE: There are many words of foreign origin in this group.

der Kuli, die Kulis   das Hobby, die Hobbys
das Auto, die Autos

PRONOUNS

PERSONAL PRONOUNS

Singular		
1st person		ich
2nd person		du
	m.	er
3rd person	*f.*	sie
	n.	es
Plural		
1st person		wir
2nd person		ihr
3rd person		sie
Formal Address		Sie

INTERROGATIVES

INTERROGATIVE PRONOUNS

wer? *who?*	**was?** *what?*

SUMMARY OF INTERROGATIVES

wann? *when?* **wie?** *how?*	**wo?** *where?* **woher** *from where?*

WORD ORDER

The verb is in first position in	*questions that do not begin with an interrogative:* Machst du Sport? Spielst du Fussball?
The verb is in second position in	*statements:* Wir spielen Tennis. Am Wochenende spiele ich Fussball. *questions that begin with an interrogative:* Woher bist du? Was spielst du gern?

VERBS

PRESENT TENSE VERB FORMS

INFINITIVES:		**spiel -en**	**mogel -n**	**find -en**	**heiss -en**
PRONOUNS		stem + ending	stem + ending	stem + ending	stem + ending
I	ich	spiel **-e**	mogl **-e**	find **-e**	heiss **-e**
you	du	spiel **-st**	mogel **-st**	find **-est**	heiss **-t**
he, she	er, sie	spiel **-t**	mogel **-t**	find **-et**	heiss **-t**
we	wir	spiel **-en**	mogel **-n**	find **-en**	heiss **-en**
you	ihr	spiel **-t**	mogel **-t**	find **-et**	heiss **-t**
they	sie	spiel **-en**	mogel **-n**	find **-en**	heiss **-en**
you (formal)	Sie	spiel **-en**	mogel **-n**	find **-en**	heiss **-en**

Note the following exceptions in the preceding chart:

a. Verbs ending in **-eln (mogeln, segeln)** drop the "e" of the ending **-eln** in the **ich**-form: **ich mogle**, and add only **-n** in the **wir-, sie-,** and **Sie**-form. These forms are always identical with the infinitive: **mogeln, wir mogeln, sie mogeln, Sie mogeln.**

b. Verbs with a stem ending in **-d** or in **-t,** such as **finden,** add **-est** in the **du**-form, and **-et** in the **er-** and **ihr**-forms: **du findest, er findet, ihr findet.**

c. All verbs with stems ending in an "s" sound **(heissen)** add only **-t** in the **du-** form: **du heisst.**

d. In speaking, the **ich-**form is often used without the ending **-e: ich spiel', ich frag'.** The omission of the **-e** is shown in writing by an apostrophe.

THE VERBS *HABEN* AND *SEIN*

	haben	sein
ich	habe	bin
du	hast	bist
er, sie, es	hat	ist
wir	haben	sind
ihr	habt	seid
sie	haben	sind
Sie	haben	sind

PRONUNCIATION

Pronunciation and reading exercises are found in the Try Your Skills
section of each unit, with the exception of the review unit.

			as in:
Kapitel (p. 53)	**1**	The **ich**-sound (/ç/)	ich, dich, Mädchen
		The **ach**-sound (/x/)	acht, achtzehn, auch
		The /l/ sound	alt, elf, Lehrer
Kapitel (p. 85)	**2**	Long vowels	da, dem, vier, du
		Short vowels: the sound /ɔ/	kosten, toll, von
		The /ü/ sound	für, fünf, Glück
		The /ö/ sound	blöd, Österreich, Wörterbuch
Kapitel (p. 113)	**3**	The sounds /R/ and /ʌ/	frei, Rad, lieber
		The diphthongs /ai/, /au/, /ɔi/	ein, sauer, neun
		The sound /ʃ/	Schule, spät, Bleistift

NUMBERS

0	null	13	dreizehn
1	eins	14	vierzehn
2	zwei	15	fünfzehn
3	drei	16	sechzehn
4	vier	17	siebzehn
5	fünf	18	achtzehn
6	sechs	19	neunzehn
7	sieben	20	zwanzig
8	acht	30	dreissig
9	neun	40	vierzig
10	zehn	50	fünfzig
11	elf	60	sechzig
12	zwölf		

ENGLISH EQUIVALENTS

The following are the English equivalents of the basic material in each section of every unit, with the exception of the review unit. They are not literal translations, but represent what a speaker of English would say in the same situation.

1 NEW FRIENDS

A1 Hello! Goodbye!
Hi, Steffi!
Hi, Andreas!
Hi, Stefan!
Hello, Michael!
Morning, Natalie!
Good morning!
Bye!
Bye! So long!
See you later!
Goodbye!

A5 Mr., Mrs., Miss
Good morning, Mr. Sperling.
Hello, Antje.

Hello, Mrs. Meier.
Hi, Michael.

Bye, Miss Seifert.
Goodbye.

B1 What's your name?
Hi! My name is Andreas. What's your name?
My name is Natalie.

And what's your name? My name is _____.

B3 What's the boy's name? What's the girl's name?
What's the boy's name?
His name is Stefan.

And the girl? What's her name?
Her name is Sabine.

B8 Who is that?
Who is that?
That's Stefan.

And who is that?
That is Mr. Sperling, the teacher.

Who is that?
That's Sabine.
And that's Mrs. Meier, the teacher.

Mr. Sperling, the German teacher.
Mrs. Meier, the German teacher

C1 How old are you?
How old are you?
I'm thirteen years old.

How old is Sabine?
Sabine is fifteen.

And how old is Stefan?
Stefan is fifteen too.

How old are Ulrike and Michael?
They are also fifteen years old.

And how old are you? I'm _____.

D1 Where are you from?
My name is Jens Kröger. I am sixteen years old. I'm from Niebüll, from Germany.

I'm Wiebke Nedel. I'm fifteen. I am also from Germany, from Neuss.

My name is Dastl, Margit Dastl. I am fourteen. I'm from Vienna, from Austria.

My name is Bruno Schmidlin. I'm fifteen. I am from Switzerland, from Zimmerwald.

I am Kurt Langer. I'm fifteen too. I'm from the DDR, from Dresden.

And where are you from? From Kansas City? From Harrisburg? Dallas? I'm from _____.

D7 Yes or no?
Jörg asks Jens:
Is your name Michael?
No, my name is Jens.
Are you from Niebüll?
Yes.

Jörg asks Lars:
Is that Jens?
Yes.
Is his name Nedel?
No, his name is Kröger.
Is he from Niebüll?
Yes, he's from Niebüll.

D13 I beg your pardon?
I'm from Liechtenstein.
From where?

What's your name?

Me? My name is . . .

That's Hans-Helmut Kurtmeyer.
I beg your pardon? Who is that?

How old is Stefan?
Stefan? —He's fifteen.

D16 What is your name? Where are you from?
Are you the German teacher?
No, I'm the math teacher.

Is your name Müller?
My name is Fischer.

Where are you from?
From Munich.

2 SCHOOL

A1 How do you get to school?
A: Look, here comes Jens on his moped!
B: Great!
A: How do you get to school?
B: Me? I come by bus. And you?
A: On foot.

Margit comes by streetcar.
Jens comes by moped.
Miss Seifert comes by car.
Wiebke comes by bike.
Who walks?

B1 School Supplies

JENS   Excuse me! How much is the dictionary, please?
SALESWOMAN   The dictionary? —Thirteen marks.
JENS   And how much is the pocket calculator?
SALESWOMAN   Eighteen marks.
JENS   I beg your pardon?
SALESWOMAN   Eighteen marks.
JENS   Great, only eighteen marks! And how much is the cassette?
SALESWOMAN   Six marks.
JENS   Thank you.
SALESWOMAN   You're welcome.

B12 How much are the school supplies? They cost . . .
books, 8 marks; pocket calculators, 18 marks;
posters, 5 marks; pencils, 1 mark;
cassettes, 6 marks; ballpoint pens, 4 marks

B20 Hey, where is the dictionary?
Hey, Jens, where is the dictionary?
It's over there. Look, Kristin, there!

Hey, Kristin, the pocket calculator's gone.
Nonsense! It's there.

Jens, where is the cassette?
Isn't it there? —Take a look, Kristin! Here it is.

Excuse me, Mrs. Meier. Where are the posters, please?
I don't know. Aren't they there?
No, they're gone.
Gone? Take a look. They are over there.

C1 Which subjects do you have today?
MRS. KRÖGER   Which subjects do you have today?
JENS   I have math, history, —wait a minute! Look, here is my class schedule. Today is Tuesday?
MRS. KRÖGER   Yes.
JENS   I have German at eight o'clock, at a quarter to nine math. Then I have English and history.
MRS. KRÖGER   When do you have physics?
JENS   On Friday.

Jens goes to high school in Niebüll. He has school from Monday to Friday. Jens has Saturdays off. School begins at eight o'clock and is over at one.

What subjects does he have? Here is Jens' class schedule.

C7 When does Jens have math?
at one o'clock / at one
at two o'clock / at two
What time is it? It is . . .
nine o'clock
nine-oh-five / five after nine
nine-ten / ten after nine
nine-fifteen / a quarter after nine
nine-twenty
nine twenty-five
nine-thirty / half past nine
nine thirty-five
nine-forty
nine forty-five / a quarter of ten
nine-fifty / ten of ten
nine fifty-five / five of ten

C10 What do you have now?
What do you have now?
We have bio now. And you?
Math. We're having a test.
Well then, good luck!

Jörg and Kristin are classmates. They are in the ninth grade, the 9a.

Mona and Lars are also classmates. They are in the ninth grade too, in the other section, the 9b.

D1 Homework and grades

Jens is doing his homework. He's doing math. In math Jens is not so good. What marks does he have in math? A four, a three, and a four. Here are Jens' grades.

KRISTIN	Hey, Jens, what do you have in German?
JENS	A two.
KRISTIN	That's great! A two in German. Fantastic!
JENS	Yes, that's good, but I only have a four in math. Dumb!
KRISTIN	Yes, that's bad. Too bad!

What do you have?
A one!
Great! Terrific!
Dumb! Too bad!

D7 Is bio hard?

Do you have a one in bio?
Yes, biology is easy.

You have algebra?
Yes.
Is algebra hard?
No, algebra isn't hard. It's easy.

3   LEISURE TIME

A1 Leisure Time: Sports and Hobbies

INTERVIEWER	What's your name?
JENS	My name is Jens.
INTERVIEWER	How old are you?
JENS	Sixteen.
INTERVIEWER	What do you do in your free time?
JENS	Well, I visit friends, I listen to music cassettes, I . . .

Jens visits friends. They listen to music cassettes.

INTERVIEWER	Do you participate in sports?
JENS	Yes. I swim and I play tennis.

Jens swims and he plays tennis.

INTERVIEWER	Do you play soccer too?
JENS	Of course!

Jens plays soccer too.

INTERVIEWER	Do you play an instrument?
JENS	Yes, I play guitar.

He plays guitar.

INTERVIEWER	Do you also have hobbies?
JENS	I collect stamps and I play chess.

Jens collects stamps.

A11 And what do you do?

INTERVIEWER	And what do you do? Do you participate in sports too?
GÜNTER	We play basketball.

The girls are sailing.
The boys are playing hockey.
The students are playing basketball.

INTERVIEWER	Do you have hobbies?
GÜNTER	Yes, I collect coins.
INTERVIEWER	And you, Kurt?
KURT	I do too.

Günter and Kurt collect coins.

The four classmates are playing cards. The game is called Mau-Mau.

INTERVIEWER	What are you playing?
KRISTIN	Mau-Mau.
INTERVIEWER	Really? Who's winning?
KRISTIN	Jens and Jörg.
JENS	As always.
KRISTIN	But you're cheating. As always.
JENS	What?! We're not cheating. You're losing and you're sore. Ha ha!

B1 When do you participate in sports?

What do you do in the summer? In fall? In the winter? In the spring?

URSEL	In the summer I play tennis and I swim.
PETER	In the fall I play soccer.
HANS	In the winter I play ice hockey and I ski.
KARIN	In the spring I play basketball.

Jörg, what do you do on the weekend?
On the weekend I play soccer.

On Sunday
on the weekend

B3 How often do you do sports?

Petra: "I seldom play tennis. Well, sometimes in the summer. In the winter I often play basketball."

Michael: "I participate in sports four times a week. Once a week, usually on Wednesday, I play tennis. On the weekend I play soccer and I swim twice a week."

once — a day
twice — a week
three times — a month
four times — a year (in the summer)

C1 Soccer is great!

INTERVIEWER   What do you do, Margit? Do you participate in sports?
MARGIT   I do gymnastics.
INTERVIEWER   Really?
MARGIT   Yes, gymnastics is fun!

INTERVIEWER   Jörg, you play soccer?
JÖRG   Yes, soccer is great.
INTERVIEWER   Do you play tennis too?
JÖRG   No. I think tennis is boring.

INTERVIEWER   Wiebke, what do you do in your free time?
WIEBKE   I read a lot.
INTERVIEWER   That's interesting. What do you read?
WIEBKE   Novels, books about sports, fantasy books . . . they're terrific!
INTERVIEWER   What do you think of comics?
WIEBKE   Dumb!

C6 True! Not true!

A: Soccer is great!
B: True!

A: How do you like the cassette?
B: Super! It's terrific!
A: Really? I think it's dumb.

A: You collect stamps?
B: Yes. Collecting is fun.
A: What? I don't think so.

A: Playing cards is boring.
B: I think so too.

A: Sailing is boring too.
B: That's not so! Sailing is great!

C10 What do you like to do?

I don't like to sail.
I like to do gymnastics.
I rather play soccer.
I like being lazy best of all.

GERMAN-ENGLISH VOCABULARY

This vocabulary includes almost all words, both active and passive, in **Neue Freunde, Erster Teil,** Units 1–4. Active words and phrases are those introduced in basic material and listed in the **Wortschatz** sections of the units. You are expected to know and be able to use active vocabulary. All other words—those appearing in the Introduction, in exercises, in optional and visual material, in the Try Your Skills and **Zum Lesen** sections, in the review unit, and in the pictorial **Landeskunde** section—are considered passive. Passive vocabulary is for recognition only. The meaning of passive words and phrases can usually be understood from context or may be looked up in this vocabulary.

With some exceptions, the following are not included: most proper nouns, and forms of verbs other than the infinitive.

Nouns are listed with definite article and plural form, when applicable. The numbers in the entries refer to the unit where the word or phrase first appears. A number in black, heavy type indicates that the word or phrase has been actively introduced in that unit. Passive vocabulary is followed by numerals in light type.

The following abbreviations are used in this vocabulary: adj (adjective), pl (plural), sing (singular), and s. th. (something).

A

ab *from, starting at,* **4**
aber *but,* **2**
die **Abkürzung, -en** *abbreviation,* **4**
acht *eight,* **1**
Achtung! *attention!,* 2
achtzehn *eighteen,* **1**
ADAC = Allgemeiner Deutscher Automobil-Club *German Automobile Club*
Algebra *algebra,* **2**
alt *old,* **1**
der **Altar, ⁻e** *altar*
das **Alter** *age,* 3
ältest- *oldest*
am: am Freitag *on Friday,* **2**; am Main *on the Main River;* am Sonntag *on Sunday,* **3**; am Tag *(times) a day,* **3**; am Wochenende *on the weekend,* **3**
amerikanisch *American* (adj), 3
an *to,* 3
die **andern** *the others,* 4
der **Anfang, ⁻e** *beginning;* Anfang Oktober *beginning of October*
das **Angebot:** unser Schul-Spezial-Angebot *our school special offer,* 2
die **Anzeige, -n** *ad,* 3
der **Artikel, -** *article* (grammar), 1; *article for a newspaper or magazine,* 2
auch *also,* **1**; ich auch *me too,* **3**
auf auf Wiedersehen! *goodbye!* **1**; schau auf die Karte! *look at the map,* 1
das **Auge, -n** *eye,* 2
aus *from,* **1**; *out, over,* **2**; *out of,* **4**; aus der Schweiz *from Switzerland,* **1**; die Schule ist aus *school's out, over,* **1**
der **Ausflugsschiff, -e** *excursion boat*
die **Ausspracheübung, -en** *pronunciation exercise,* 1
auswählen (sep) *to choose, select,* 2
das **Auto:** mit dem Auto *by car,* **2**
der **Autor, -en** *author,* 3

B

der **Bäcker, -** *baker,* 1
die **Badener Weinstrasse** *scenic road winding through the wine-growing region of the state of Baden*
die **Banane, -n** *banana*
Basel *Basel,* **1**
Basketball *basketball,* 3
das **Bauernbrot, -e** *dark peasant bread*
der **Baum, ⁻e** *tree*
beginnt *begins,* **2**
begrüssen *to greet*
Belgien *Belgium,* 1
der **Berg, -e** *mountain*
das **Bergsteigen** *mountain climbing*
Bern *Bern,* 1
besuchen *to visit,* **3**; Freunde besuchen *to visit friends,* **3**
das **Bierzelt, -e** *tent at a beer festival or carnival where you drink beer and eat*
das **Bild, -er** *picture,* 2

das **Bilder-Quiz** *picture quiz,* 3
die **Bio** *short for* Biologie, **2**
die **Biologie** *biology,* **2**
bis *to,* 6; bis dann! *see you later,* **1**; von . . . bis *from . . . to,* **1**
bisher *until now,* 2
bist: du bist *you are,* **1**
bitte *please,* **2**; *you're welcome,* **2**
der **Bleistift, -e** *pencil,* **2**
der **Blick, -e** *view;* mit Blick auf *with a view of*
blöd *stupid, dumb,* **2**
BMW = Bayerische Motorenwerke *Bavarian Motor Works* (BMW is a German-made car)
der **Bodensee** *Lake Constance*
das **Braunkohlenwerk, -e** *brown-coal mine*
BRD = Bundesrepublik Deutschland *Federal Republic of Germany,* 1
der **Brief, -e** *letter,* **1**
der **Brieffreund, -e** *pen pal,* **1**
die **Briefmarke, -n** *stamp,* **3**
das **Briefmarkensammeln** *stamp collecting,* **3**
der **Büchermuffel, -** *person who doesn't like books,* **3**
die **Buchhandlung, -en** *book store,* **4**
die **Bundesrepublik** *Federal Republic,* 1
die **Bundesrepublik Deutschland** *Federal Republic of Germany,* 1
der **Bus:** mit dem Bus *by bus,* **2**
der **Butt, -e** *flounder,* 3

C

die **Comics** (pl) *comics,* **3**
der **Computer, -** *computer,* **3**
das **Computerspiel, -e** *computer game,* **3**
die **Confiserie, -n** *candy shop*

D

da *there; here,* **2;** da drüben *over there,* **2;** da kommt *here comes,* **2**
das **Dach, ¨er** *roof*
Dänemark *Denmark,* **1**
danken: danke! *thanks! thank you!* **2**
dann *then,* **2**
das *the; that,* **1;** das ist *that is,* **1**
DDR = Deutsche Demokratische Republik *German Democratic Republic,* **1**
das **Deckenfresco, -ken** *ceiling fresco*
der *the,* **1**
das **Deutsch** *German (language),* **2**
die **Deutsche Demokratische Republik** *German Democratic Republic,* **1**
Deutschland *Germany,* **1**
der **Deutschlehrer, -** *German teacher (m),* **1**
die **Deutschlehrerin, -nen** *German teacher (f),* **1**
dich *you (sing),* **1**
die *the,* **1**
der **Dienstag, -e** *Tuesday,* **2**
dir: wie steht's mit dir? *What about you?* **2**
DM *abbreviation for Deutsche Mark,* **2**
der **Donnerstag, -e** *Thursday,* **2**
dort *there,* **2;** dort drüben *over there,* **2**
das **Drachenfliegen** *hang gliding,* **3**
dran: jetzt bist du dran *now it's your turn,* **1**
drei *three,* **1**
dreimal *three times,* **3**
dreissig *thirty,* **2**
dreizehn *thirteen,* **1**
die **Dressur** *training*
drüben: da drüben *over there,* **2;** dort drüben *over there,* **2**
dtv = Deutscher Taschenbuch Verlag *German paperback publisher*
du *you (sing),* **1;** du, . . . *hey, . . . ,* **2**

E

ehemalig *former*
der **Eigentümer, -** *owner*
ein, eine *a, an,* **2, 3**
einfach *simple, easy,* **1**
einige *several, some,* **3**
einmal *once,* **3**
eins *one,* **1;** eine Eins *a one (see note, p 51),* **2**
das **Eishockey** *ice hockey,* **3**
das **Eistanzen** *ice dancing,* **3**
elf *eleven,* **1**

F

das **Elsass** *Alsace-Lorraine*
englisch *English (adj),* **4**
Englisch *English (language),* **2**
Entschuldigung! *excuse me,* **2**
er *he; it,* **2**
die **Erdkunde** *geography,* **4**
erinnern an *to commemorate*
die **Erklärung, -en** *explanation,* **1**
erzählen: erzähl mal *tell,* **2**
es *she; it,* **2**
Europa *Europe,* **1**

F

das **Fach, ¨er** *subject,* **2**
das **Fachwerkhaus, ¨er** *half-timbered house*
das **Fantasy-Buch, ¨er** *fantasy book,* **3**
faulenzen *to lie around, be lazy,* **3**
feiern *to celebrate*
der **Feiertag, -e** *holiday*
der **Festspielort, -e** *town having a festival or pageant*
die **Festung, -en** *fortress*
die **Figur, -en** *figure,* **3**
das **Finanzzentrum, -zentren** *financial center*
finden *to find, think, have the opinion about s.th.,* **3;** das finde ich nicht *I don't think so,* **3;** wie findest du . . . ? *how do you like . . . ? what do you think of . . . ?* **3**
der **Fischer, -** *fisherman,* **1**
der **Fischerhafen, ¨** *fishing port*
fliessen *to flow*
der **Fluss, ¨e** *river*
der **Fotoapparat, -e** *camera*
Franken *Franconia*
fränkisch: die Fränkische Schweiz *Franconian Switzerland (part of Franconia having many lakes)*
Frankreich *France,* **1**
die **Frau, -en** *Mrs.,* **1**
das **Fräulein, -** *Miss,* **1**
frei *off,* **2;** er hat frei *he has off, he has no school,* **2**
der **Freitag, -e** *Friday,* **2**
die **Freizeit:** in deiner Freizeit *in your free time,* **3**
das **Fresko, Fresken** *fresco*
der **Freund, -e** *friend,* **3**
Frl. = Fräulein *Miss,* **1**
das **Frühjahr** *spring,* **3;** im Frühjahr *in the spring,* **3**
die **Fuggerei** *trading company run by the Fugger family in the 16th century*
fünf *five,* **1**
fünfunddreissig *thirty-five,* **2**
fünfundfünfzig *fifty-five,* **2**
fünfundvierzig *forty-five,* **2**
fünfundzwanzig *twenty-five,* **2**
fünfzehn *fifteen,* **1**
fünfzig *fifty,* **2**
der **Fuss:** am Fusse *at the foot of;* ich komme zu Fuss in die Schule *I walk to school,* **2;** zu Fuss *on foot,* **2**
Fussball *soccer,* **3**

G

gar: gar nicht *not at all,* **3**
der **Gärtner, -** *gardener,* **1**
die **Gastfamilie, -n** *host family*
das **Geburtshaus, ¨er** *house of birth*
die **Gedächtniskirche, -n** *Memorial Church*
die **Geigenbauerstadt, ¨e** *town of violin makers*
die **Geographie** *geography,* **2**
gerade *just now, at the moment,* **3**
gern *gladly,* **3;** gern (machen) *to like (to do),* **3;** nicht gern (machen) *to not like (to do),* **3**
die **Geschichte, -n** *history,* **2**
die **Gesellschaft, -en** *society*
gewinnen *to win,* **3**
die **Gitarre, -n** *guitar,* **3**
das **Glück** *luck; viel Glück good luck!* **2**
GmbH = Gesellschaft mit beschränkter Haftung *company with limited liability*
der **Gott:** Gott bring mich durch diesen Tag! *God, let me survive this day!* **4;** Gott sei Dank! *Thank God!* **5**
grösst- *biggest*
der **Gruss, ¨e:** viele Grüsse *best regards,* **1**
grüss dich! *hi!* **1**
gut *good,* **2;** guten Morgen! *good morning!* **1;** guten Tag! *hello!* **1;** hör gut zu! *listen carefully,* **1**
das **Gymnasium, Gymnasien** *type of German secondary school,* **2**
die **Gymnastik:** Gymnastik machen *to do gymnastics,* **3**

H

haben *to have,* **2**
haha! *ha ha!* **3**
halb: halb zehn *nine-thirty,* **2**
hallo! *hi!* **1**
der **Halm, -e** *blade, piece*
hätte *would have*
die **Hausaufgaben** (pl) *homework,* **2;** er macht Hausaufgaben *he's doing homework,* **2**
die **Hausfassade, -n** *house front*
das **Heft, -e** *notebook,* **2**
die **Heide, -n** *heath, moor*
die **Heidschnucke, -n** *moorland sheep*
die **Heimat** *home*
heissen *to be called,* **1;** er heisst Jens *his name is Jens,* **1;** ich heisse *my name is,* **1;** wie heisst du? *what's your name?* **1**
der **Herbst** *fall,* **3;** im Herbst *in the fall,* **3**
Herr *Mr.,* **1**
heute *today,* **2**
hier *here,* **1**
der **Hintergrund** *background*
das **Hobby, -s** *hobby,* **3**
höchster: Deutschlands höchster Berg *Germany's highest mountain*

die **Hochzeit, -en** *wedding*
Hockey *hockey,* **3**
das **Holstentor** *Holsten Gate*
hören *to listen,* **3**; hör gut zu!
Listen carefully! **1**
das **Hörspiel, -e** *radio play*
der **Hubschrauber, -** *helicopter,* **2**

I

ich *I,* **1**; ich? *me?* **1**
identifizieren *to identify,* **4**
ihr *you* (pl), **2**
immer *always,* **3**
in *in,* **2**
das **Instrument, -e** *instrument,* **3**
interessant *interesting,* **3**
das **Interview, -s** *interview,* **3**
der **Interviewer, -** *interviewer,* **3**
ist *is,* **1**

J

ja *yes,* **1**
das **Jahr:** im Jahr *(times) a year,* **3**
das **Jahreszeugn.** = Jahreszeugnis, -se
report card, **1**
das **Jahrhundert, -e** *century*
die **Jeans-Tasche, -n** *denim bag,* **2**
jetzt *now,* **2**
der **Junge, -n** *boy,* **1**

K

der **Kaiser:** der Wilde Kaiser *mountain
range in Tirol*
das **Kapitel, -** *chapter,* **1**
die **Karte, -n** *map,* **1**; *card,* **3**; Karten
spielen *to play cards,* **3**
das **Kartenspielen** *playing cards,* **3**
das **Karwendelgebirge** *Karwendel
Mountains*
die **Kassette, -n** *cassette,* **2**
kehrt: zurückkehren (sep) *to return,* **4**
die **Kerze, -n** *candle*
klar: na klar! *well, of course!* **3**
die **Klasse, -n** *class; grade,* **2**; Klasse!
great! **3**
die **Klassenarbeit, -en** *test,* **2**
der **Klassenkamerad, -en** *classmate,* **2**
das **Klassenprojekt, -e** *class project,* **1**
das **Klavier, -e** *piano,* **4**
kommen *to come,* **2**
korrespondieren *to correspond,* **4**
der **Körper, -** *body,* **4**
kosten *to cost,* **2**; was kosten?
how much are? **2**
kostet: was kostet? *how much is?* **2**
die **Kreditbank** *bank*
der **Kuli, -s** *ballpoint pen,* **2**
die **Kunst** *art,* **2**
der **Kurort, -e** *health resort town*

L

der **Laden, -** *store,* **2**
die **Lampe, -n** *lamp*
das **Land, -er** *country,* **1**

die **Landeskunde** *culture,* **1**; ein
wenig Landeskunde *a little culture,* **1**
langsam *slowly,* **4**
langweilig *boring,* **3**
Latein *Latin,* **2**
das **Leben** *life,* **4**; langsam kehrt Leben
in meinen Körper zurück *slowly
life is returning to my body,* **4**
der **Lehrer, -** *teacher* (m), **1**
die **Lehrerin, -nen** *teacher* (f), **1**
leicht *easy,* **2**
lernen *to learn,* **3**
lesen *to read,* **3**
das **Lesen** *reading,* **3**; zum Lesen *for
reading,* **1**
die **Leseübung, -en** *reading exercise,* **1**
lieber (machen) *to prefer (to do),* **3**;
ich spiele lieber Fussball *I'd rather
play soccer,* **3**
lieber (m), liebe (f) *dear,* **3**
das **Lieblingsfach, -er** *favorite subject,*
4
liebsten: am liebsten (machen) *to
like (to do) most of all,* **3**
Liechtenstein, *Liechtenstein,* **1**
liegen *to lie,* **1**
liest: was liest du? *what do you
read?* **3**
literarisch *literary*
der **Lücken-Dialog, -e** *dialog with
blanks to be filled in,* **3**
der **Luftkurort, -e** *high-altitude or mountain resort*
die **Lüftlmalerei** *the tradition of paint-
ing scenes on houses*

M

machen *to do,* **3**; was machst du?
What are you doing? What do you do? **3**
macht: er macht Mathe *he's doing
math,* **3**
das **Mädchen, -** *girl,* **1**
man: man spricht Deutsch *German is spoken,* **1**; wie sagt man das?
How do you say that? **1**
manchmal *sometimes,* **3**
die **Mark, -** *mark* (German monetary
unit), **2**; eine Mark *one mark,* **2**;
eine Mark zehn *one mark and 10
pennies,* **2**; zwei Mark *two marks,* **2**
der **Marktplatz, -e** *marketplace*
die **Maske, -n** *mask*
die **Mathe** *math,* **1**
das **Mathematikbuch, -er** *math book*
der **Mathematiklehrer, -** *math teacher,*
1
Mau-Mau *card game similar to
crazy eights,* **3**
die **Meinung, -en** *opinion,* **3**
meistens *mostly,* **3**
mit: mit dem Auto *by car,* **2**; mit
dem Bus *by bus,* **2**; mit dem
Moped *on (his) moped,* **2**; mit
dem Rad *by bicycle,* **2**; mit der
Strassenbahn *by streetcar,* **2**

der **Mitschüler, -** *classmate* (m), **1**
mitten in *in the middle of,* **1**
der **Mittwoch** *Wednesday,* **2**
mogeln *to cheat,* **3**
der **Moment:** Moment mal! *wait a
minute!* **2**
der **Monat:** im Monat *(time) a month,* **3**
der **Montag** *Monday,* **2**
das **Moped, -s** *moped,* **2**; mit dem
Moped *on (his) moped,* **2**
der **Morgen:** Morgen! *morning!* **1**
der **Müller,-** *miller,* **1**
München *Munich,* **1**
die **Münze, -n** *coin,* **3**
die **Musik** *music,* **2**
die **Musikkassette, -n** *music cassette,*
3; Musikkassetten hören *to listen
to music cassettes,* **3**

N

na *well,* **2**; na klar! *of course!* **3**
nach *after, past,* **2**
der **Nachbar, -n** *neighbor,* **1**
der **Name, -n** *name,* **2**
nein *no,* **1**
neu *new,* **1**; neue Freunde *new
friends,* **1**
der **Neubau, -ten** *new building*
neun *nine,* **1**
neunzehn *nineteen,* **1**
nicht *not,* **2**
nie *never,* **3**
die **Niederlande** (pl) *the Netherlands,*
1
noch: was machen sie noch? *what
else do they do?* **3**
das **Nordfriesenhaus, -er** *North Frisian house*
Norditalien *Northern Italy,* **1**
nördlich *north,* **1**
die **Nordseeinsel, -n** *island in the
North Sea*
die **Note, -n** *grade, mark,* **2**
null *zero,* **1**
nur *only,* **2**

O

das **Oberland** *highland*
die **Oberschule, -n** *high school,* **2**; er
geht auf die Oberschule *he goes to
high school,* **2**
oder *or,* **1**
oft *often,* **3**
der **Opernball, -e** *opera benefit ball*
das **Original:** im Original *in the original (language),* **3**
Ost *East,* **1**
Österreich *Austria,* **1**
ostfriesisch *East Frisian*
Ostfriesland *East Frisia*
östlich *east,* **1**

P

die **Parallelklasse, -n** *class of the same
grade,* **2**

der **Partner, -** *partner,* 1
die **Partnerarbeit** *teamwork,* 1
passen *to fit,* 2
die **Pause, -n** *break, recess,* 2
die **Pflanze, -n** *plant*
phantastisch *fantastic, great,* 2
philosophieren *to philosophize,* 3
Physik *physics,* 2
populär *popular,* 3
das **Poster, -** *poster,* 2
die **Postkarte, -n** *postcard,* 1
der **Preis, -e** *price,* 2
prima! *great!* 2
das **Promenadenkonzert, -e** *concert on a promenade*

R

das **Rad;** mit dem Rad *by bike,* 2
raten *to guess,* 1; rat mal! *take a guess!* 1
das **Ratespiel, -e** *guessing game,* 1
das **Rathaus, ⁻er** *city hall,* 4; am Rathaus *next to the city hall,* 4
die **Rathausfassade, -n** *front of the city hall*
rausziehen (sep) *to pull out*
die **Realschule, -n** *type of German secondary school,* 4
reduziert *reduced,* 2
das **Reetdach, ⁻er** *thatched roof*
die **Reitschule, -n** *riding school*
die **Reklame, -n** *ad,* 2
die **Religion,** *religion,* 2
die **Residenz, -en** *(prince's) residence*
das **Rheinland** *Rhineland*
das **Rollenspiel,** *role-playing,* 2
der **Roman, -e** *novel,* 1
die **Ruhe:** in Ruhe *not rushed,* 2

S

sammeln *to collect,* 3
das **Sammeln** *collecting,* 3
der **Samstag** *Saturday,* 3
sauer *sore, annoyed,* 3
Schach *chess,* 3
schade! *too bad!* 2
der **Schäfer, -** *shepherd*
der **Schaffner, -** *fare collector*
die **Schallplatte, -n** *record,* 4
schauen: schau! *look!* 2; schau auf die Karte! *look at the map,* 1; schau mal! *look! take a look!* 2
Schi: ich laufe Schi *I go skiing,* 3
das **Schilaufen** *skiing*
schlecht *bad,* 2
schreiben *to write,* 1; bitte schreib mir! *please write to me,* 1; wer schreibt uns? *who will write to us?* 3
die **Schreibgeräte** (pl) *writing instruments,* 2
die **Schreibübung, -en** *writing exercise,* 1
die **Schreibwaren** (pl) *writing supplies,* 4
das **Schreibwarengeschäft, -e** *stationery store,* 2
der **Schuhmacher, -** *shoemaker,* 1

der **Schulanfang** *beginning of school,* 2
die **Schule, -n** *school,* 2
der **Schüler, -** *student, pupil,* 3
die **Schülerzeitung, -en** *school newspaper,* 2
die **Schulsachen** (pl) *school supplies,* 2
die **Schultasche, -n** *school bag,* 2
der **Schulweg** *way of getting to school,* 4
die **Schulwoche** *the school week,* 4
Schwaben *Swabia*
der **Schwarzwald** *Black Forest*
Schwarzwälder: Schwarzwälder Schinken *Black Forest ham*
die **Schweiz** *Switzerland,* 1
schwer *difficult,* 2
schwimmen *to swim,* 3
das **Schwimmen** *swimming,* 3
sechs *six,* 1
sechzehn *sixteen,* 1
sechzig *sixty,* 2
segeln *to sail,* 3
das **Segeln** *sailing,* 3
seit *since*
selten *seldom,* 3
sie *she, it; they,* 2
Sie *you* (formal), 1, 3
sieben *seven,* 1
siebzehn *seventeen,* 1
so *so,* 2
das **Sofa, -s** *sofa*
der **Sommer, -** *summer,* 3; im Sommer *in the summer,* 3
der **Sonnabend** *Saturday,* 2
sonnabends *Saturdays, on Saturdays,* 2
der **Sonntag** *Sunday,* 3
sonst: ein Tag wie sonst *a day like any other,* 3
die **Sozialwohnung, -en** *government-supported housing*
spanisch *Spanish* (adj)
der **Spass** *fun,* 3; Gymnastik macht Spass *gymnastics is fun,* 3
spät: wie spät ist es? *what time is it?* 2
das **Spiel, -e** *game,* 3
spielen *to play,* 3
Spitze! *terrific!* 3
der **Sport** *gym,* 2; Sport machen *to participate in a sport, to do sports,* 3
der **Sport- und Hobbyfreund, -e** *sport and hobby enthusiast,* 3
der **Sport- und Hobbymuffel, -** *person who doesn't like sports or hobbies,* 3
das **Sportbuch, ⁻er** *book about sports,* 3
die **Sprache, -n** *language,* 3; der deutschen Sprache *of the German language,* 3
sprechen *to speak, talk,* 3
sprich: sprich mich nicht an! *don't talk to me,* 3
spricht: man spricht Deutsch *German is spoken,* 1
stattfinden (sep) *to take place*
stattgefunden: hat stattgefunden *took place*

der **Steckbrief, -e** *resumé,* 4
stehen: wie steht's mit dir? *what about you?* 2
sterben *to die,* 4; lieber Gott, lass mich sterben! *dear God, let me die!* 4
stimmt: stimmt! *that's right! true!* 3; stimmt nicht! *that's not so! not true!* 3
das **Stövchen, -** *candle warmer*
die **Strasse, -n** *street,* 3
die **Strassenbahn:** mit der Strassenbahn *by streetcar,* 2
St. = Stück *piece, item,* 4; Bleistifte (10 St.) *10 pencils,* 4
das **Stück, -e** *piece, item,* 2
der **Stundenplan, ⁻e** *class schedule,* 2
südlich *south,* 1
Südtirol *South Tyrol,* 1
super! *super! terrific!* 3

T

der **Tag, -e** *day,* 3; am Tag *(times) a day,* 3; guten Tag! *hello!* 1; Tag! *hello! hi!* 1
täglich *daily, every day,* 3
das **Tanzen** *dancing,* 4
der **Taschenrechner, -** *pocket calculator,* 2
das **Teeservice, -** *tea set, service*
der **Teil, -e** *part,* 1
die **Telefonnummer, -n** *telephone number,* 1
das **Tennis** *tennis,* 3
Tirol *Tyrol*
tja *hm* 3
toll! *great!* 2
die **Tracht, -en** *traditional costume*
der **Treffpunkt, -e** *meeting place*
das **Treppenhaus, ⁻er** *staircase*
tropisch *tropical*
tschau! *bye! so long!* 1
die **Tschechoslowakei** *Czechoslovakia,* 1
tschüs! *bye! so long!* 1
typisch *typical*

U

die **U-Bahn** = Untergrundbahn *subway,* 4; mit der U-Bahn *by subway,* 4
das **Üben** *practice, practicing,* 1
über *about,* 1
die **Übung, -en** *exercise, activity, practice,* 1
die **Uhr, -en** *clock, watch,* 1; neun Uhr dreissig *nine-thirty,* 2; neun Uhr fünf *nine-oh-five,* 2; neun Uhr zehn *nine-ten,* 2
der **Uhrmacher, -** *watchmaker*
um *at,* 2; um acht Uhr *at eight o'clock,* 2; um eins *at one,* 2
die **Umfrage, -n** *survey, poll,* 3
der **Umzug, ⁻e** *parade*
und *and,* 1
die **Universitätsstadt, ⁻e** *university town*
unmöglich *impossible,* 2

die **Unordnung** *mess, disorder,* **2**; so eine Unordnung! *what a mess!* **2**
uns *us,* **3**
der **Unsinn:** Unsinn! *nonsense!* **2**

V

verbrannt *burned*
die **Vereinigten Staaten** (pl) *United States,* **1**
die **Verkäuferin, -nen** *salesperson,* **2**
verlieren *to lose,* **3**
versteckt: versteckte Sätze *hidden sentences,* **3**
viel *much, a lot,* **3**; viel Glück! *good luck!* **2**
viele: viele Grüsse *best regards,* **1**
vier *four,* **1**
viermal *four times,* **3**
das **Viertel:** Viertel nach neun *a quarter after nine,* **2**
vierzehn *fourteen,* **1**
vierzig *forty,* **2**
das **Volksfest, -e** *fair, festival*
von *by,* **3**; von . . . bis *from . . . to,* **1**
vor *before, of,* **2**; *in front of, outside of*
der **Vorname, -n** *first name,* **1**
der **Vortrag, ¨e** *presentation,* **2**
VW = Volkswagen *a German-made car*

W

wann? *when?* **2**

was? *what?* **2**; was?! *what?!* **3**; was kosten? *how much are?* **2**; was kostet? *how much is?* **2**; was machst du? *what are you doing? what do you do?* **3**
die **Waschmaschine, -n** *washing machine*
weg *gone,* **2**
der **Weinberg, -e** *vineyard*
das **Weinfest, -e** *wine festival*
die **Weinstrasse, -n** *road through wine-growing villages*
weiss: ich weiss nicht *I don't know,* **2**
welche *which, what,* **2**
der **Weltatlas, -se** *world atlas,* **4**
wenig: ein wenig *a little,* **1**
wer? *who?* **1**
Westfalen *Westphalia*
westlich *west,* **1**
wie *such as,* **3**; wie? *how?* **1**; wie bitte? *I beg your pardon?* **1**; wie heisst du? *what's your name?* **1**; wie immer *as always,* **3**; wie kommst du in die Schule? *how do you get to school?* **2**; wie oft? *how often?* **3**; wie spät ist es? *what time is it?* **2**
das **Wiederholungskapitel, -** *review unit (chapter),* **4**
das **Wiedersehen:** auf Wiedersehen! *goodbye!* **1**; Wiedersehen! *bye!* **1**
Wien *Vienna,* **1**
das **Windsurfen** *wind surfing,* **3**

der **Winter** *winter,* **3**; im Winter *in the winter,* **3**
wir *we,* **2**
wirklich? *really?* **3**
wo? *where?* **2**
die **Woche:** in der Woche *(times) a week,* **3**
woher? *from where?* **1**; woher bist du? *where are you from?* **1**
das **Wohnhaus, ¨er** *house*
der **Wohnsitz, -e** *residence*
das **Wörterbuch, ¨er** *dictionary,* **2**
der **Wortschatz** *vocabulary,* **1**
die **Wortschatzübung, -en** *vocabulary exercise, practice,* **1**
würde *would*

Z

die **Zahl, -en** *number,* **1**
zehn *ten,* **1**
die **Zeit** *time,* **2**
die **Zeitschrift, -en** *magazine,* **3**
der **Zensurenspiegel** *grade record,* **2**
zu: zu Fuss *on foot,* **2**
Zürich *Zurich,* **1**
zurückkehren (sep) *to return,* **4**
zwanzig *twenty,* **1**
zwei *two,* **1**
zweimal *twice,* **3**
zwischen *between,* **1**
zwölf *twelve,* **1**

ENGLISH-GERMAN VOCABULARY

This vocabulary includes all the words in the **Wortschatz** sections of **Neue Freunde, Erster Teil,** Units 1–4. These words are considered active—you are expected to know them.

Idioms are listed under the English word you would be most likely to look up. German nouns are listed with definite article and plural ending, when applicable. The number after each German word or phrase refers to the unit in which it is first introduced. To be sure of using the German words and phrases in correct context, refer to the units in which they appear.

A

a *ein,* 3; *eine,* 2
after *nach,* 2
algebra *Algebra,* 2
also *auch,* 1
always *immer,* 3; as always *wie immer,* 3
am: I am *ich bin,* 1
an *ein,* 3; *eine,* 2
and *und,* 1
are: you are *du bist,* 1; they are *sie sind,* 1
art *die Kunst,* 2
at *um,* 2; at eight o'clock *um acht Uhr,* 2; at one *um eins,* 2
Austria *Österreich,* 1

B

bad *schlecht,* 2; too bad! *schade!* 2
ballpoint *der Kuli, -s,* 2
basketball *Basketball,* 3
before *vor,* 2
begin *beginnen,* 2
bicycle *das Rad, -er,* 2; by bicycle *mit dem Rad,* 2
bio *Bio,* 2
biology *Biologie,* 2
book: book about sports *das Sportbuch, -er,* 3
boring *langweilig,* 3
boy *der Junge, -n,* 1
bus *der Bus, -se,* 2; by bus *mit dem Bus,* 2
but *aber,* 2
by: by bicycle *mit dem Rad,* 2; by bus *mit dem Bus,* 2; by car *mit dem Auto,* 2; by moped *mit dem Moped,* 2; by streetcar *mit der Strassenbahn,* 2
bye! *tschau!* 1; *tschüs!* 1; *Wiedersehen!* 1

C

calculator: pocket calculator *der Taschenrechner, -,* 2
car: by car *mit dem Auto,* 2
cards *die Karten* (pl), 3
cassette *die Kassette, -n,* 2; music cassette *die Musikkassette, -n,* 3

cheat *mogeln,* 3
chess *Schach,* 3
class *die Klasse, -n,* 2; class of the same grade *die Parallelklasse, -n,* 2
classmate (m) *der Klassenkamerad, -en,* 2
classmate (f) *die Klassenkameradin, -nen,* 2
coin *die Münze, -n,* 3
collect *sammeln,* 3
collecting *Sammeln,* 3
come *kommen,* 2
comics *Comics* (pl), 3
cost *kosten,* 2

D

day *der Tag, -e,* 3; (times) a day *am Tag,* 3
dictionary *das Wörterbuch, -er,* 2
difficult *schwer,* 2
do *machen,* 2, 3; he's doing math *er macht Mathe,* 2; What are you doing? *was machst du?* 3; what do you do? *was machst du?* 3
dumb *blöd,* 2

E

easy *leicht,* 2
English *Englisch,* 2
excuse: excuse me! *Entschuldigung!* 2

F

fall *der Herbst,* 3; in the fall *im Herbst,* 3
fantastic *phantastisch,* 2
fantasy book *das Fantasy-Buch, -er,* 3
find *finden,* 3
foot: on foot *zu Fuss,* 2
four *vier;* four times *viermal,* 3
free time *die Freizeit,* 3; in your free time *in deiner Freizeit,* 3
Friday *der Freitag,* 2; on Friday *am Freitag,* 2
friend *der Freund, -e,* 3
from *aus,* 1; *von* 1
fun *der Spass,* 3; gymnastics is fun *Gymnastik macht Spass,* 3

G

game *das Spiel, -e,* 3
geography *Geographie,* 2
German (language) *Deutsch,* 2
German (person) *der Deutsche, -n,* 2
German Democratic Republic *Deutsche Demokratische Republik (DDR),* 1
Germany *Deutschland,* 1
get: how do you get to school? *wie kommst du in die Schule?* 2
girl *das Mädchen, -,* 1
gone *weg,* 2
good *gut,* 2; good luck! *viel Glück!* 2
goodbye! *auf Wiedersehen!* 1
good morning! *guten Morgen!* 1
grade *die Note, -n,* 2; *die Klasse, -n,* 2
great! *prima!* 2; *toll!* 2; *Klasse!* 3
guitar *die Gitarre, -n,* 3
gymnastics *Gymnastik,* 3; to do gymnastics *Gymnastik machen,* 3

H

he *er,* 2
hello! *hallo!; Tag!; guten Tag!* 1
here *hier,* 2; here comes *da kommt,* 2
hey, . . . *du, . . .,* 2
hi! *grüss dich!; hallo! Tag!* 1
high school *die Oberschule, -n,* 2; he goes to high school *er geht auf die Oberschule,* 2
history *Geschichte,* 2
hm *tja,* 3
hobby *das Hobby, -s,* 3
hockey *Hockey,* 3
homework *die Hausaufgaben* (pl), 2; he's doing homework *er macht Hausaufgaben,* 2
how *wie,* 1; how much are . . .? *was kosten . . .?* 2; how much is . . .? *was kostet . . .?* 2; how often? *wie oft?* 3; how old are you? *wie alt bist du?* 1

I

ice hockey *Eishockey,* 3
in *in,* 2; they're in the ninth grade *sie gehen in die neunte Klasse,* 2

instrument *das Instrument, -e,* 3
interesting *interessant,* 3
interviewer *der Interviewer, -,* 3
is: he is *er ist,* 1; she is *sie ist,* 1
it *er,* 2; *sie,* 2; *es,* 2

K

know: I don't know *ich weiss nicht,* 2

L

Latin *Latein,* 2
lazy: to lie around, be lazy *faulenzen,* 3
like: to like (to do) *gern (machen),* 3; to like (to do) most of all *am liebsten (machen),* 3; to not like (to do) *nicht gern (machen),* 3; how do you like . . .? *wie findest du . . .?* 3
listen (to) *hören,* 3
look: look! *schau!* 2; *schau mal!* 2
lose *verlieren,* 3
lot: a lot *viel,* 3
luck: good luck! *viel Glück!* 2

M

mark *die Note, -n,* 2; *die Mark,* 2
math *Mathe,* 2
math teacher *der Mathematiklehrer, -,* 2
me? *ich?* 1; me too *ich auch,* 3
minute: wait a minute! *Moment mal!* 2
Miss *Fräulein,* 1
Monday *der Montag, -e,* 2; on Monday *am Montag,* 2
month *der Monat, -e,* 3; (times) a month *im Monat,* 3
moped *das Moped, -s,* 2; by moped *mit dem Moped,* 2
most: to like (to do) most of all *am liebsten (machen),* 3
mostly *meistens,* 3
Mr. *Herr,* 1
Mrs. *Frau,* 1
much *viel,* 3
Munich *München,* 1
music *die Musik,* 2
music cassette *die Musikkassette, -n,* 3

N

name *der Name, -n,* 2; his name is *er heisst,* 1; my name is *ich heisse,* 1; her name is *sie heisst,* 1; what's . . . name? *wie heisst . . .?* 1; is your name . . .? *heisst du . . .?* 1
never *nie,* 3
nine *neun,* 1; nine-thirty *halb zehn,* 2
ninth grade *die neunte Klasse,* 2
no *nein,* 1
nonsense! *Unsinn!* 2
not *nicht,* 2; to not like (to do) *nicht gern (machen),* 3
notebook *das Heft, -e,* 2
novel *der Roman, -e,* 3
now *jetzt,* 3
number *die Zahl, -en,* 1; the numbers from zero to twenty *die Zahlen von null bis zwanzig,* 1; the numbers from 5 to 60 *die Zahlen von 5 bis 60,* 2

O

of: a quarter of nine *Viertel vor neun,* 2; of course! *na klar!* 3
off *frei;* he has off, he has no school *er hat frei,* 2
often *oft,* 3; how often? *wie oft?* 3
old *alt,* 1
once *einmal,* 3
one *eins,* 2; (the grade of) one *eine Eins,* 2
only *nur,* 2
opinion: to have the opinion about *finden,* 3
or *oder,* 1
out *aus,* 2; school is out *die Schule ist aus,* 2
over *aus,* 2; school is over *die Schule ist aus,* 2; over there *da drüben,* 2

P

pardon: I beg your pardon? *wie bitte?* 1
past: five past nine *fünf nach neun,* 2
pen (ballpoint) *der Kuli, -s,* 2
pencil *der Bleistift, -e,* 2
physics *Physik,* 2
play *spielen,* 3
playing cards *Kartenspielen,* 3
please *bitte,* 2
pocket calculator *der Taschenrechner, -,* 2
poster *das Poster, -,* 2
prefer *lieber,* 3; to prefer (to do) *lieber (machen),* 3
pupil *der Schüler, -,* 3

Q

quarter: a quarter after nine *Viertel nach neun,* 2

R

rather *lieber,* 3; I'd rather play soccer *ich spiele lieber Fussball,* 3
read *lesen,* 3; what do you read? *was liest du?* 3
really: really? *wirklich?* 3
recess *die Pause, -n,* 2
religion *Religion,* 2
right: that's right! *stimmt!* 3

S

sail *segeln,* 3
sailing *Segeln,* 3
salesperson *die Verkäuferin, -nen,* 2
Saturday *der Samstag, -e,* 3; *der Sonnabend, -e,* 2; on Saturday *am Sonnabend,* 2; (on) Saturdays *sonnabends,* 2
schedule: class schedule *der Stundenplan, ¨e,* 2
school *die Schule, -n,* 2; high school *die Oberschule, -n,* 2; he goes to high school *er geht auf die Oberschule,* 2; how do you get to school? *wie kommst du in die Schule?* 2
school supplies *die Schulsachen* (pl) 2
see: see you later! *bis dann!* 1

seldom *selten,* 3
she *sie; es,* 2
ski: I go skiing *ich laufe Schi,* 3
so *so,* 2; so long! *tschüs! tschau!* 2
soccer *Fussball,* 3
sometimes *manchmal,* 3
sore *sauer,* 3
spring *das Frühjahr,* 3; in the spring *im Frühjahr,* 3
sport *der Sport,* 3; sports *der Sport,* 3; to participate in a sport, to do sports *Sport machen,* 3
stamp *die Briefmarke, -n,* 3
streetcar *die Strassenbahn, -en,* 2; by streetcar *mit der Strassenbahn,* 2
student *der Schüler, -,* 3
stupid *blöd,* 2
subject *das Fach, ¨er,* 2
summer *der Sommer, -,* 3; in the summer *im Sommer,* 3
Sunday *der Sonntag, -e,* 3; on Sunday *am Sonntag,* 3
super! *super!* 3
swim *schwimmen,* 3
Switzerland *die Schweiz,* 1; from Switzerland *aus der Schweiz,* 1

T

teacher *der Lehrer, -* (m), 1; *die Lehrerin, -nen* (f) 1; German teacher *der Deutschlehrer, -,* 1
tennis *Tennis,* 3
terrific! *Spitze!* 3
test *die Klassenarbeit, -en,* 2
thank: thank you *danke,* 2
thanks *danke,* 2
that *das,* 1; that's . . . *das ist . . .* 1
the *der, die, das,* 1
then *dann,* 2
there *da, dort,* 2; over there *da drüben, dort drüben,* 2
they *sie,* 2
think *finden,* 3; I don't think so *das finde ich nicht,* 3; what do you think about . . .? *wie findest du . . .?* 3
three *drei,* 3; three times *dreimal,* 3
Thursday *der Donnerstag,* 2; on Thursday *am Donnerstag,* 2
time: free time *die Freizeit,* 3; in your free time *in deiner Freizeit,* 3; what time is it? *wie spät ist es?* 3
times: three times *dreimal,* 3; four times *viermal,* 3
today *heute,* 2
too: me too *ich auch,* 3
true! *stimmt!* 3; not true! that's not so! *stimmt nicht!* 3
Tuesday *der Dienstag,* 2; on Tuesday *am Dienstag,* 2
twice *zweimal,* 3

V

Vienna *Wien,* 1
visit *besuchen,* 3

W

wait: wait a minute! *Moment mal!* 2

we *wir,* 2

Wednesday *der Mittwoch,* 2; on Wednesday *am Mittwoch,* 2

week: (times) a week *in der Woche,* 3

weekend *das Wochenende, -n,* 3; on the weekend *am Wochenende,* 3

welcome: you're welcome *bitte,* 2

well *na,* 2

what? *was?* 2; *welche?* 2; **what?!** *was?!* 3

when? *wann?* 2

where? *wo?* 2; from where? *woher?* 1; where are you from? *woher bist du?* 1

who? *wer?* 1; who's that? *wer ist das?* 1

win *gewinnen,* 3

winter *der Winter, -,* 3; in the winter *im Winter,* 3

Y

year *das Jahr, -e,* 1; thirteen years old *dreizehn Jahre alt,* 1; (times) a year *im Jahr,* 3

yes *ja,* 1

you *du,* 1; *Sie* (formal), 1; *ihr, Sie* (pl), 2

GRAMMAR INDEX

ABBREVIATIONS

def	*definition*		pron	*pronoun(s)*
plur	*plural*		ques	*question(s)*
pres	*present*		sing	*singular*

address: **du**-form, 93; **ich**-form, 93; **wir**-form, 98; **ihr**-form, 98; **Sie**-form, 51, 99

am liebsten: 107

article: *see* definite article

class: def, 39

definite article: to identify gender, 39, 66

gender: def, 39, 66

gender marker: def, 66

gern: 107

haben: pres tense forms of, 76

infinitive: def, 99

kommen: pres tense forms of, 63

lieber: 107

nouns: classes of, 39; gender, 66; plur of, 68

noun phrases: referred to by pron, 71

present tense: of **sein,** 43; of **kommen,** 63; of **haben,** 76; sing and plur, 99; of **spielen,** 99

pronouns: personal pron, 43; **er, sie, es,** and **sie** (plur), 71

questions: asking and giving names, 37; asking and answering ques, 48; ques anticipating a yes or no answer, 49; ques beginning with a verb, 49; **was kostet, was kosten,** 69

question words: ques beginning with a ques word, 48

sein: pres tense forms of, 43

tense: pres, 99

verbs: **was kostet, was kosten,** 69; **du**-form, 93; **ich**-form, 93; **ihr**-form, 98; **wir**-form, 98

verb-second word order: 103

word order: verb in second place, 103

B
C
D 1
E 2
F 3
G 4
H 5
I 6
J 7